Mr. Dickey's BARBECUE COOKBOOK

To

VANESSA

Roland Dickey

Mr. Dickey's BARBECUE COOKBOOK

Recipes from a True Texas Pit Master

Roland Dickey

with
Polly Powers Stramm

photography by **Robert M. Peacock**

PELICAN PUBLISHING COMPANY
Gretna 2014

First printing, September 2012
Second printing, January 2014

Produced by Pinafore Press, Janice Shay
Photography by Robert M. Peacock
Styling and props by Denise Gee, Laura Dickey
Production assistant, Paige Blackorby
Recipe testing and preparation, Jeff Forrester
Assistant editor, Sarah Jones
Index, Sara LeVere
Photograph, back cover, by Tres Watson

ISBN: 9781455616862
E-book ISBN: 9781455616879

Printed in China
Published by Pelican Publishing Company, Inc.
1000 Burmaster Street, Gretna, Louisiana 70053

This book is dedicated to my lifelong partner and brother,
T.D. Dickey Jr. He and I built Dickey's together
for over 40 years without one cross word.
T.D.—See you on the other side.

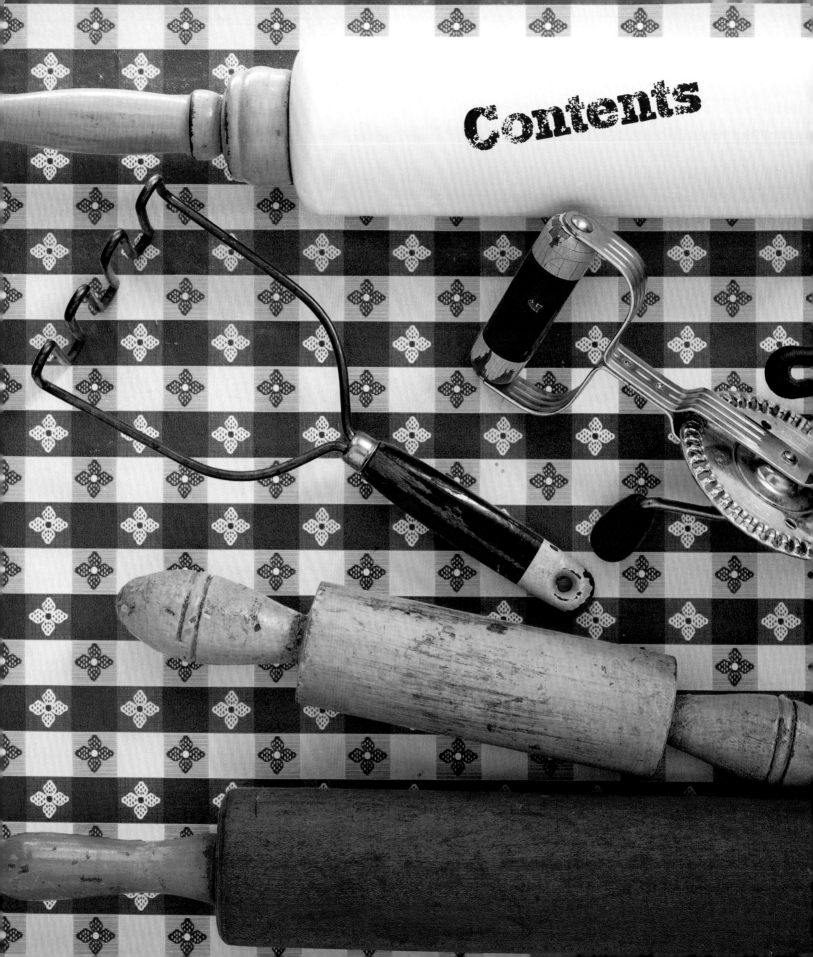

Contents

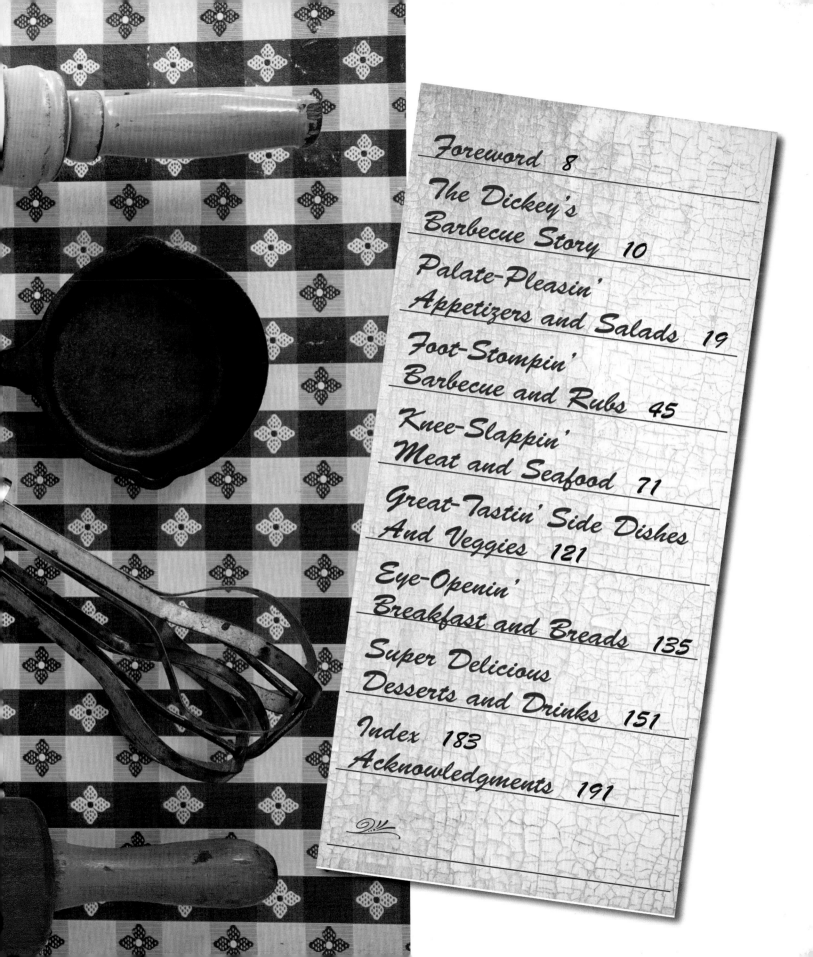

Foreword

DICKEY'S BARBECUE IS PLENTY MORE THAN JUST TEXAS-STYLE BARBECUE with all the fixin's. Dickey's is the colorful story of a hardworking American family—from Travis Dickey who opened "store number one" in Dallas in 1941 to Roland Dickey Jr. who runs the super-successful operation today. In between, and still very much in the picture, is Roland Dickey Sr., the face of Dickey's and part of the close-knit family that took over the business in the 1960s after their father's untimely death.

Roland Dickey Sr. is truly a one-of-a-kind character who adores cooking and entertaining. He also is quite a raconteur whose wife calls him a cross between Jackie Gleason and Rodney Dangerfield. Perhaps that's why he has appeared on the "Regis and Kelly" show and has starred in knee-slapping YouTube and television commercials with a zany woman nicknamed Edna.

Unbeknownst to him, Roland was cultivating a knack for business while working alongside his mom and dad in the original Dickey's in north Dallas. But like George Bailey, the character in the classic movie "It's a Wonderful Life," Roland was itching to leave the family business behind for greener pastures. What Roland didn't realize way back when was that happiness—and success—can be found right in your own backyard, as trite as it may sound.

Throughout the pages of this book, Roland tells stories that you'll share at the supper table or entertain your neighbor with over the backyard fence. He offers popular, never-before-published recipes from Dickey's, including Momma's Mac (and cheese), as well as dozens of favorites that were fine tuned in his family's kitchen. In addition to recipes, Roland offers his personal philosophy on cooking (as well as other topics), time-saving tips, and his take on what every smart cook should have on hand in their pantry. Roland also dishes on everything from what kind of wine to drink while cooking to a combination of spices that he reverently calls "the trinity"—onions, bell peppers, and celery.

Roland Dickey's life lessons make this book a must for every kitchen or coffee table. You'll want to get comfortable on the sofa, prop your feet up, leaf through the pages and find out what Roland Dickey has to say next.

—*Polly Powers Stramm*

The Dickey's Barbecue Story

EVEN THOUGH I WAS PRACTICALLY RAISED BESIDE THE PIT at Dickey's Barbecue in north Dallas, Texas, I never intended to be in the restaurant business. It may come as a surprise to some folks but when I was growing up, I was pretty darn sure that I wanted to be a lawyer. As a child in the 1950s, I contracted polio, spent a lot of time indoors and often was a fill-in at my mother's bridge table. Thank goodness I suffered no lasting effects from polio but while I was laid up and not playing cards, I zeroed in on TV's "Perry Mason." I watched actor Raymond Burr, who played old Perry, strut into the courtroom and tackle all those intriguing cases with the help of his beautiful assistant Della Street.

Looking back, I figure my dad, Travis Dickey Sr., was typical in that he wanted his children to have a better life than he did. Dad only had a seventh or eighth grade education but his business sense was razor sharp. He spent years at Dickey's getting to know lawyers, doctors and other well-dressed professionals who were regulars at the restaurant. I truly believe he wanted that kind of life for his sons. He hoped that each of us would land a job with an honest-to-goodness office and an air-conditioned car. But a traditional career, as such, was not meant to be, although in high school and college my long-range plan was to become a criminal lawyer or a dashing Hollywood agent.

I love talking about Dickey's Barbecue, which now has nearly 250 stores, because it is a true American success story. It all started with the opening of the first Dickey's—store number one, as we've always called it—in 1941 on the eve of the United States' involvement in World War II. Dad was a one-of-a-kind character who was blessed with a gift of gab that took him far and wide. He was born and raised on a farm in east Texas and, in 1917, left straight from there to fight in World War I. After the war ended, Dad—like most soldiers of that era—had to wait for room on a ship to bring him back to the states. As a result, he ended up living in France for several months before he had a spot on a ship. I think his experience in France gave him both a sense of adventure and the courage that would influence him for the rest of his life. His time in France also led him to eventually open Dickey's Barbecue, although that pivotal moment happened years later.

Dad finally made it back to the good old U.S. of A. and headed West to sow a few wild oats. Can you imagine going back to a farm after you've seen the bright lights of "Paree?" Nope, the farm wasn't the life for my Dad. First, he had to go exploring. For the next decade—those carefree Roaring '20s—Dad worked various jobs in California. Probably the most interesting time for him was the five years that he managed a soda fountain at Hollywood Boulevard and Vine Street. I've seen snapshots of Dad taken in those days and I can only imagine how exciting his life was at that point.

Shortly after the Great Depression hit, Dad came down with a bout of homesickness and returned to Texas. My grandparents, meanwhile, had felt the economic pinch and lost the farm. They moved to Dallas and opened a greasy spoon called J.P.'s Café. Dallas became Dad's home base and it wasn't long before he met an attractive secretary named Ollie Rich and was married. For the next few years Dad worked a series of jobs that kept food on the table for him and Mom. He was a versatile guy and was hired to operate a beer distributorship and work at a convenience store, among other jobs. Deep down inside, though, I think Dad knew he wanted to be his own boss. One day while driving around north Dallas, Dad spotted a beat-up, former beer joint. He really had a vision and reckoned he could make a purse out of a sow's ear, so to speak. The beer joint was at the intersection of Knox and Central, near the old central railroad tracks with dirt roads bordering either side. In later years, the old railroad tracks became the North Dallas Expressway—also known as Interstate 75, one of two major traffic arteries in central Dallas.

Dad knew how to smoke meat so he figured that he would transform that tired looking beer joint into a barbecue stand. He opened the first Dickey's on October 15, 1941, and called it a stand because

The original Dickey's Barbecue in 1946. My dad, Travis Dickey, with my sister, Elizabeth, and my brother T. D.

it was basically a counter with stools. Eventually, he put in a few school desks but never in his lifetime had tables and chairs in that location. For sentimental reasons, we keep a row of the original school desks in store number one.

In the beginning, Dickey's truly was a one-man operation. Dad cooked, waited on customers and cleaned up. Sandwiches were 10 cents, which was about the price of a gallon of gas. Funny how today's sandwich prices also mirror the price of a gallon of gas. Since day one we have had a reasonably priced menu because we know people are always on the lookout for good, inexpensive food.

During busy times, Mom helped Dad by carrying sandwiches to customers' cars. One December day, Mom was running sandwiches outside when a car radio blared out the news about the bombing of Pearl Harbor. She had no idea where Pearl Harbor was but she and the customer figured that it must be in Hawaii. Like a lot of folks, they also couldn't imagine why anyone would want to bomb America.

No doubt about it, World War II changed the nature of Dad's business. Suddenly everyone was working at least one and possibly two jobs, and they had money to eat out. Almost overnight, the country became prosperous. Rationing also began and the amount of meat my father could buy was limited to the rationing coupons he was issued. Turns out, he only had enough food to be open for

five days a week and often sold out of meat. During this boom in business, my parents finally could afford to hire employees. They added two people to the payroll but continued to work tirelessly. They also started a savings account. As a matter of fact, when the war ended, my parents had enough money tucked away to buy the property on which the business was located. All along they had been paying $50 a month in rent and Dad was satisfied with that arrangement. But, like the true Capricorn and sure-footed business woman that she is, Mom prevailed. My parents paid $5,000 for the land, which probably seemed like a fortune. Through the years, the property values have increased so much that if my parents hadn't bought that piece of land, they eventually wouldn't have been able to afford to put a Dickey's on it.

Meanwhile, Mom and Dad had three children—my sister, Elizabeth Mills, my late brother, T.D. (for Travis Dickey Jr.) and me. I came along in 1947 when Dad was 50. Thankfully there was no birth control then because if there had been, I may have been just a glimmer in my Dad's eye. Growing up, Dickey's Barbecue couldn't help but be a part of our lives. As a youngster, I made $1 a week rolling tamales, bussing tables, making sandwiches and doing this 'n that. Yes siree, I rolled more than my share of hot tamales on Saturday mornings at the restaurant. We don't serve

Above: Two original customers waiting for lunch outside the restaurant, 1941. Below: My dad at the original store serving barbecue to the mayor of Dallas.

tamales anymore but the original machine is on display at one of our stores. It's memorabilia like this that gives Dickey's that good old down-home feeling.

When I was a teenager, Dickey's employed a couple of colorful characters named Red and Lee who both carried firearms to work. I guess they thought they'd be ready to shoot it out with anybody who tried to rob the place. After the lunch rush, Red and I would grab a sandwich and a glass of milk or a bottle of Dr. Pepper, and sit in the back of the store where Red would entertain me with stories of the Dallas he knew as a boy.

Of course, I couldn't help but put in my two cents worth. Anyone who has ever met me might describe me as an energetic guy who could probably talk the stripes off a zebra. So, when I was younger, it came as no surprise that I would become a member of the debate team both in high school in Dallas and in college at Southern Methodist University. And when it comes to getting in front of a camera, I'm certainly not shy. I enjoy the heck out of making corny commercials and YouTube videos for Dickey's. I won't ever forget how much fun I had as a guest on "Regis and Kelly" in New York. But going to Hollywood or being in show business just wasn't in the cards for me.

In 1966 I was a student at SMU living at home in Dallas. That was the agreement I had with my parents—they would pay my tuition if I lived with them and worked at Dickey's. Deep down inside, I still wanted to be a lawyer.

I woke up from that dream one day in 1967 when I experienced a real-life nightmare and got the call that every child dreads. Dad was only 69, but had dropped dead of a heart attack while sitting at one of the school desks in store number one. Mind you, Dad never drank alcohol but I don't ever remember him not having a cigarette in his hand. Cigarettes probably killed him because he averaged between 80 and 100 a day. He picked up smoking during World War I when an Army doctor told him it was good for his throat. He tried to quit several times but never kicked the habit. Dad never made a lot of money, but he worked hard for what we had. He simply made a living. It might not be what some consider to be a nice living but we had a home and plenty to eat.

When Dad died, my brother and I stopped what we were doing

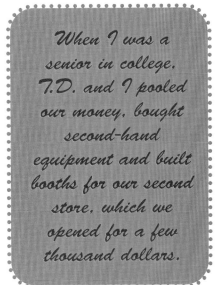

When I was a senior in college, T.D. and I pooled our money, bought second-hand equipment and built booths for our second store, which we opened for a few thousand dollars.

and took over the business because we wanted to help Mom. Everything soon worked out for the best, which is how I think things always do. I'm often asked how Dickey's began and I explain it this way: Dad opened the barbecue stand, and my brother and I turned Dickey's into a restaurant and started the business.

I was only the second person in my family to attend college. My brother, T.D., graduated from SMU nearly 10 years before I started. As a freshman I joined the debate team because I had the itch to travel and the team competed in tournaments at other colleges throughout the South. When I was growing up my family had neither the money nor time to take vacations, so the debate team seemed like my ticket to see other cities. As it happened, the team also was responsible for a blossoming romance between me and a pretty girl named Maurine Petty. She was a junior and I was a freshman so ordinarily she wouldn't have given me the time of day. But I was a debater so I eventually persuaded her to go out with me. After a lot more debating, we were married in August 1967. I was 20 and she was a 22-year-old recent graduate of SMU.

I was still taking classes when Maurine became the breadwinner for our family. She was hired as a social worker for the Texas Welfare Department. For the first few years of our marriage, we lived exclusively off Maurine's $400 monthly salary. It wasn't until September 1968 when I opened the second Dickey's location with my brother that Maurine and I made more than her pittance of a salary. She literally supported us in the beginning, which made it possible for me to put everything I had into making a second Dickey's Barbecue work. If Maurine hadn't been ready, willing and able to support us, we never would have expanded the business. (By the way, Big Momma is the affectionate name I use to refer to my wife of more than 40 years of wedded bliss.)

When I was a senior in college, T.D. and I pooled our money, bought second-hand equipment and built booths for our second store, which we opened for a few thousand dollars. I convinced every business connection I had at the original Dickey's to give us just enough credit to get that second location up and running. It was a huge gamble that paid off. With all that going on, I even graduated from SMU in four years.

We chose Garland, Texas, for a second location because I had done

Top: Roland Dickey doing a radio program for 99.5 Wolf. Above: Roland giving a cooking demonstration with host Rebecca Miller of NBC 5 television.

OK. If not, we were probably out of the barbecue business for good.

On opening day I chopped barbecue, my brother was in the kitchen and Maurine may have been running the cash register. After helping me get started with our second location, Maurine concentrated on her social work career. She went on to run the child welfare program for the state of Texas under Governor Bush. She also is a former chair of the Parkland Health and Hospital System's Board of Visitors, in addition to a long list of other impressive appointments. In 2004 she decided to run for county commissioner of district one in Dallas. She won and is serving her second term as a Dallas County Commissioner. Now, in addition to calling her Big Momma, I refer to her as "the commissioner."

Turns out, in our family, cooking has always been a male effort. Big Momma has made an art of not cooking. In fact, I've never even told her where the stove is. Dad cooked, my brother and I cook, and my oldest son Roland Jr. now runs the company, and likes to grill and make simple foods like I do. My youngest son Cullen, who works for a commercial real estate outfit and handles real estate for Dickey's, is a gourmet cook. He once told me that he was so inspired by my cooking that he became the primary cook in his own family. In Cullen's words: "My father's passion for different ethnic cuisines and tremendous culinary creativity encouraged us to love cooking."

How about that?!

Starting when Roland and Cullen were about seven or eight years old, I would take them to work with me on weekends. I was anxious for both boys to understand the value of a dollar and to develop a good work ethic. After all, as a kid I had worked in the restaurant with my Dad and rolling tamales for a quarter was how I learned the business. On Saturday afternoons, the boys stood on milk cartons in the kitchen to peel potatoes or scrape carrots.

Roland Jr. has always loved the restaurant business and kept his summer job at Dickey's all the way through high school. After he graduated from SMU, Roland knew he wanted to stay in the business but I had a brainstorm. I wanted him to make his own way. I told him he had to go to work for another restaurant and become successful on his own before we'd talk about other options. Roland embraced that idea and, upon graduation, went to work for El Chico, a Dallas-based Tex-Mex chain of about 75 restaurants. He worked his way up from kitchen manager and became El Chico's youngest general manager to date.

When El Chico's offered Roland yet another promotion, it was the right time for me to counter. Knowing that everyone would assume I had "given" him a job, I also made him work his way up at Dickey's. He started out as a general manager of a Dickey's that was

a little research and knew that it was a town that had a good lunch business. By day, I ran the original Dickey's and at night, I would jump in the car and drive to the second location to get it ready to open. When that day came, we had just enough credit for a supply of a week's worth of food. When the doors opened, it was one of those life-changing moments. We knew that if the gamble paid off we'd be opening in New Mexico. He understood that he had to make that restaurant successful before he could move up in the company. He did and worked in Dickey's operations before first becoming vice president, and finally president and chief executive officer.

Since he was named president, Roland has more than doubled the size of the company—twice. I am extremely proud of his hard work and dedication to making the family business a success. I also am thrilled that he has taken the barbecue business farther than I could have imagined, while also maintaining the integrity of our food.

Roland also has continued another family tradition. He met his wife Laura in Dallas and they married in 2006. Naturally, he's the cook in their household.

Cullen, meanwhile, decided the restaurant business wasn't for him. After he graduated from SMU, he chose commercial real estate as his future endeavor. His first and only real estate boss, so far, is David Little, who has been a fantastic mentor for Cullen. During the 1980s, David was our across-the-street neighbor, so it was great to see Cullen go to work for him. I'm proud as punch that Cullen has become a successful real estate broker while maintaining a passion for cooking and food. He met his wife, Allison, at SMU and they were married in 2005. It's funny. Like most Dickey men, Cullen is chief cook and bottle wash at home.

With Dickey's expanding every day, I was fortunate enough to be able to give my sons a lot more than I had while growing up in the 1950s and '60s. Back then, most people wanted to eventually own a Cadillac. When I was young, my parents never drove anything except second-hand Chevrolets. One of my dreams was to own a Cadillac. In 1971 my brother and I found ourselves making that dream come true. Being good ole Southern boys, we first bought our mother a brand spanking new Cadillac on credit for a three-year payout. In 1974, we traded it in for another new Cadillac for her and two Cadillacs for each of us. I have never felt more

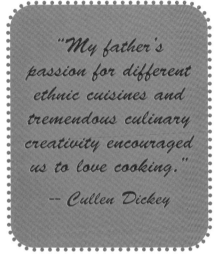

"My father's passion for different ethnic cuisines and tremendous culinary creativity encouraged us to love cooking."
-- Cullen Dickey

successful as I did when I could afford a new Cadillac. Of course in this day and age, talk like that sounds unsophisticated, but when I was a working-class kid coming up, the definition of success was simple: a new car for Mom and a new car for you. If you really made it, that car was a Cadillac, the car of every Texan's dreams.

Hanging in every one of our Dickey's restaurants is an old photo of my brother, my mom and me standing in front of store number one with those two Cadillacs parked in front of us. The picture was taken the day we bought the cars. We display that photo in all the restaurants because, to us, it truly symbolizes success.

After that, I added a few other philosophies to my list of what I measure as success. After buying a Cadillac, I wanted to get to the point in my life where I would be able to afford NOT to eat leftovers. While growing up, we always had to eat leftovers and we had to eat them until they were gone, even if that meant eating the same thing for two or three days. Now, I'm proud to say that Maurine and I can afford to do away with leftovers. They don't go to waste, though. We give them as treats to one of our three dogs. I know the leftover thing is not a big deal to some people, but to me, not eating leftovers is a real measure of success.

Another way I deem myself as successful is looking at a restaurant menu and not worrying about the right-hand column—where the prices are listed. My parents hardly ever took us to restaurants and, during the first years of our marriage, Big Momma and I would only go out to eat if we had clipped a coupon or if we knew the restaurant had a reasonable special. When Maurine and I finally could go out to eat and not look at the prices, we knew we had truly arrived.

Our family has come a long way and, of course, so has Dickey's Barbecue. Materialistically speaking, not having a lot when I was young, I realized a long time ago just how important it was to make Dickey's Barbecue a good value. My brother and I certainly wanted the

Roland Dickey with sons Cullen and Roland Jr., at the Brown Derby restaurant in Las Vegas in 2001.

restaurant to be a big hit, but we also wanted it to be a fair deal. We always were looking for ways to add value for the customer, which brings me to another funny story. One time my brother and I were at a fancy steakhouse in Austin, Texas. The servers brought a big block of complimentary cheese to each table for customers to enjoy during the meal. Everybody loved it and that reaction made a huge impression on us. We copied the idea and put out a block of cheese at each Dickey's so each guest could slice their own cheese. The cheese was popular for a few years but local health departments began having second thoughts. Number one, the cheese sat around uncovered, and secondly, people were slicing the cheese with a sharp knife. We had to lose the cheese but ended up offering free pickles and ice cream, not necessarily together unless a pregnant woman had a craving.

Dickey's stores have changed slightly through the years. Store number one is still owned by our family and continues to be open for business. In fact, it is the oldest, continually operating restaurant in Dallas. It has never moved, changed its name or closed its doors. Yep, the menu certainly has evolved through the years. We started with beef brisket and smoked ham on white bread. Pickles and potato chips came on the side and a carton of milk washed it all down. Since then, we've expanded the menu to include eight smoked meats and 12 sides. We still smoke all our meats in a genuine hickory wood pit on-site at each and every Dickey's location. Smoking meats on-site is important because people have tons of different ideas about barbecue. For example, is it better to smoke it over hickory wood, apple wood or cherry wood? Or do you dry rub meat with spices before smoking? The list could go on and on. But, the flavor of meat that has been smoked over wood in a pit or on a grill never can be replaced. Even our highest volume Dickey's never has strayed from our signature way of smoking meats overnight.

Our highest volume store ever was built on what once was considered to be the edge of Dallas. Today that neighborhood is known as the galleria area of North Dallas. That store, which we owned and operated for nine years, opened in 1975. We lost it in 1984 and I say

Roland Dickey and wife, Maurine (Big Momma).

'lost' because that area grew so fast, the city of Dallas eventually decided the road near the store had to be widened. In order to do so, the city took in the nearly two acres that we owned—store included—to expand the Dallas North Tollway. Our building was leveled to make way for more people. The city paid us for the land, but there was no way to truly replace that store. That particular Dickey's was one of the city's most popular lunch spots. An odd thing about that store was the bank of pay phones I had put in when we built the restaurant. Naturally, this was long before everyone had even heard of a cell phone so men needed a pay phone if they had to call a business associate during lunch. The bank of pay phones coupled with the restaurant's location, at the far edge of the city's northward expansion, made this particular Dickey's THE place for lunch in Dallas.

The longer I was in the restaurant business the more I learned about cooking. With the barbecue stand, Dad cooked as much as Mom did when I was growing up. By the time I was nine, I was a whiz at washing raw vegetables, peeling potatoes, scraping carrots and, of course, rolling tamales. I also was quite an expert at seasoning food and smoking meats, but that wasn't until I was ten. By the time my brother and I were running Dickey's I had been looking for better food, more options and new recipes. I think Yuppies would describe me as a "foodie," but I just consider what I do as learning the business. I'm always reading—at least two books a week—and I'm forever developing recipes. I spend a ton of time on the road visiting our stores, attending grand openings and hamming it up on radio broadcasts or TV commercials. I also enjoy visiting other restaurants wherever I go because I love good food.

A few years ago the Dallas Morning News printed an article with the headline, "Wife's Political Career Ends Husband's Cooking Show." Maurine had just announced her intentions of running for the county commission and I was doing a morning cooking segment for a local television show called "Good Morning Texas." Maurine's political contest was heated and the network big shots were concerned that the network's election coverage wouldn't seem fair if they were evaluating her

Travis Dickey II, Director; eldest son, Roland Dickey Jr., President/CEO; Roland Dickey; the late T.D. Dickey; youngest son Cullen Dickey, Director of Real Estate.

on the evening news while I was on in the morning. After the newspaper article came out, a local radio station, "The Wolf" called me. The Wolf had the most popular morning radio show in Dallas and he asked me to do a weekly cooking segment. The show found it hilarious that my wife's political ambitions had abruptly ended my TV show. I had a howling good time for a couple of years cooking on the show at the Wolf.

"Starring" in so many cooking segments that targeted folks at home really has pushed me to develop recipes that work in a normal kitchen. Those TV and radio segments also have been instrumental in my seeing to fruition the cookbook idea that I have dreamed of for ages. I've discovered that cooking in a commercial kitchen with large quantities of food and specialized equipment is far different than what will work in a home kitchen. How many backyards are equipped with a commercial grade gas barbecue pit that smokes 600 pounds of meat all at once? Not many, for sure. I know for certain that the recipes in this book will work because they are based on my personal collection. You'll certainly see a few items in this book that are similar to the ones we serve at Dickey's but the recipes aren't exactly the same.

We serve fast-casual food at Dickey's. It's good food that's not too expensive and fast, and in the pages of this book you will find tips on how to do just that. These days, most every family is on a tight schedule with both parents usually working outside the home. Sandwiched in between Mama and Daddy's beat-the-clock day are kids'

Back row: Roland Jr., Cullen's wife Allison, Cullen, and Roland Dickey. In front: Roland Jr.'s wife Laura and Maurine Dickey (Big Momma).

activities like sporting events and practices, music and dance lessons, and everything else. Working parents who usually handle meal preparation for the family simply don't have an hour or two at the end of a weekday to spend precious time in the kitchen.

I'm a big believer in cooking being fun, not time-driven. So have both a good time reading this book and cooking for your family and friends. Life is too short not to make the most of it. ✴

Pickled Shrimp

This dish is so good that my family won't stop eating it. My wife, Big Momma, likes to eat this recipe with crackers as her main course. She doesn't want to waste any time with any other course besides this one. I always buy my shrimp raw, peel and de-vein them myself, and boil them with a little crab seasoning, water, and beer. No matter how you get the shrimp, remember, use Gulf shrimp if at all possible—not imports.

Serves 4, or double the recipe to serve 8 to 10

1 pound raw Gulf shrimp, cooked, peeled, and de-veined
½ cup chopped green onions, tops and bottoms
3 cloves garlic, chopped and mashed
½ cup chopped celery

Marinade
1 lemon
½ cup olive oil
1 tablespoon chili sauce, or ketchup
1 tablespoon Louisiana hot sauce
1 tablespoon white vinegar
1 teaspoon paprika
Salt, to taste
Pepper, to taste
1 teaspoon Cajun seasoning (optional)

Stir together the shrimp, onions, garlic, and celery in a bowl.

In a separate bowl, combine all the marinade ingredients and whisk together. Pour the marinade over the shrimp, place in a tightly covered plastic storage container, and refrigerate overnight.

Prior to serving, drain the shrimp in a small colander to get rid of the excess vinegar and oil. Discard the excess marinade. Set the shrimp out with toothpicks to skewer.

Original Potato Salad

Serves 4 to 6

5 pounds russet potatoes
½ cup mayonnaise
¼ cup sugar
2 tablespoons white vinegar
½ cup sweet relish
¼ cup diced red peppers
1 cup Kraft cole slaw dressing
¼ cup diced celery
Kosher salt, to taste
Finely ground black pepper, to taste

Preheat the oven to 225 degrees F.

Wash the potatoes under cool running water, pat dry, place them on a sheet tray, and bake for 70 to 90 minutes. Remove the potatoes from the oven, place them in a dish towel, and remove and discard the skins while the potatoes are warm. Chop the potatoes into 1-inch pieces and place them into a bowl.

In a separate bowl, combine the mayonnaise, sugar, vinegar, relish, peppers, dressing, and celery and whisk until well incorporated. Add this mixture to the bowl of potatoes and stir well using a spatula, until the salad is mixed but still has small chunks of potatoes. Season to taste with salt and pepper. Refrigerate, covered, for 4 to 6 hours before serving.

Chili Con Queso

Yields about 3 cups

1 large block Velveeta cheese
4 ounces half-and-half
1 (8-ounce) can Rotel peppers, with juice
1 teaspoon chili powder
1 diced tomato, for garnish
Jalapeños, sliced, for garnish

Melt the block of Velveeta cheese and the half-and-half in a saucepot or double boiler over medium heat, stirring occasionally and being careful not to burn the cheese or cream. Add the Rotel peppers and juice, and continue to heat. Stir in the chili powder and chopped tomatoes. Stir over the heat until all of the ingredients are thoroughly combined and heated through.

Garnish with jalapeños to taste and serve hot with tortilla chips.

You can buy chili con queso already made and all you have to do is melt it. On the other hand, it's extremely simple to make it from scratch.

Mexican Party Dip

This dip is served warm or hot and it's excellent for a cocktail party. Don't bring it out until the last minute before serving. Be sure to have lots of tostados handy. Once the folks start eating this, they won't stop. It's that good!

Serves 4 to 6

2 cans refried beans
12 to 14 jalapeño peppers, sliced
1 pint chili con queso (see recipe, p. 25), or use store-bought
4 ripe avocados, sliced
3 tomatoes, chopped

Preheat the oven to 350 degrees F.

Layer a 9 x 13-inch baking dish with 1 inch of refried beans. Cover the refried beans completely with jalapeño pepper slices. Spoon the chili con queso over the beans to cover. Decorate the top with a few more sliced jalapeños.

Bake uncovered for 30 to 40 minutes. Remove from the oven and layer the avocados and tomatoes on top of the chili con queso, and serve immediately.

Note: If you're concerned about this dish being too spicy, you can always serve the jalapeño peppers on the side.

Midori Melon and Ham Salad

Serves 4 to 6
Cook Time: 5 to 7 minutes

1 honeydew melon, husk removed, halved and seeded
4 ounces Midori liquor
3 tablespoons fresh mint, chopped
10 to 15 slices Prosciutto ham, sliced paper thin

Using a 1-inch melon baller, scoop out about 40 melon balls and place them inside a large plastic zip-top bag. Add the Midori and 1 tablespoon mint to the bag and seal. Chill for 3 hours.

Preheat the oven to 405 degrees F.

Place a roasting rack inside a sheet tray, and lay the Prosciutto slices on the roasting rack. Bake the Prosciutto for 5 to 7 minutes, or until crispy. Remove from the oven, let cool at room temperature, then chop the Prosciutto into small pieces.

Remove the melon balls from the refrigerator and push a skewer into the end of each ball to make a "lollipop." Roll the melon skewers in the chopped Prosciutto to cover. Arrange the skewers on a platter, and sprinkle with the remaining chopped mint. Serve chilled.

This recipe is a lot more sophisticated than the name sounds. It is great to serve on a hot evening as an appetizer or first course.

Idiot Sticks

This goofy name came from a friend of mine that invented this recipe. Knowing him like I do, the name fits. A combination of salt and bacon in your mouth is delicious with drinks. Even people who are not idiots love this goofy appetizer.

Serves 4 to 6

**1 (16-ounce) package large salt pretzel sticks, the thickness of a large pencil
12 strips bacon, thinly sliced**

Preheat the oven to 350 degrees F.

Wrap each pretzel with a strip of raw bacon. Place the pretzels on a cookie sheet and bake for 30 to 40 minutes, or until the bacon is completely cooked and crisp. The time may vary due to the thickness of the bacon and the thickness of the pretzels, so check them often.

A TIP I like to share involves the pantry and refrigerator and what any cook should have on hand at all times. I call it my emergency list because if friends drop in unexpectedly you can throw together an appetizer or even dinner.

For the pantry:
- *A carton each of beef stock and chicken stock (Pacific or Progresso brands)*
- *Canned albacore tuna*
- *Sliced black olives*
- *Pitted pimento-stuffed green olives*
- *Tomatoes, celery, onions and peeled garlic*
- *Olive oil (unfiltered)*
- *Pasta*
- *Fresh lemons*
- *Canned condensed milk*
- *Canned tomatoes*
- *Bread crumbs*
- *White rice (I prefer Rice-Tec brand, which happens to be grown in Texas)*

For the refrigerator:
- *Real mayonnaise*
- *Peeled raw garlic*
- *Bacon*
- *Parmesan Cheese*

Stuffed Mushrooms

There is nothing easier to make than a stuffed mushroom. Every time I make these for people, all the mushrooms get eaten. They are specifically designed to go with cocktails or wine.

Serves 4 to 6

12 large mushroom caps, stems removed
2 links Italian sausage, preferably spicy

Preheat the oven to 225 degrees F.

Wash the mushroom caps and pat dry.

Slit open the casing of the two sausage links, remove the sausage, and chop it up. Using your hands, stuff each mushroom cap with the raw Italian sausage. Place in a baking dish or a sheet pan and bake for about 30 minutes. Mild sausage can be substituted if you desire less heat.

Mom's Cranberry Salad

My mom loved cranberries in anything, and so do I.

Serves 4 to 6

2 cups sugar
1 pound fresh cranberries, ground in a food processor
1 cup miniature marshmallows
1 cup chopped pecans
1 (9-ounce) can crushed pineapple, drained
1 cup whipped cream

Stir the sugar into the ground cranberries and let stand at room temperature for 30 minutes. Stir in the marshmallows, pecans, and pineapple. Stir in the whipped cream last. For best results, make this salad one day ahead. Refrigerate before serving.

Old-Fashioned Dill Potato Salad

Serves 4 to 6
Cook Time: 70 to 90 minutes

5 pounds russet potatoes
¾ cup sour cream
¾ cup mayonnaise
¼ cup fresh dill sprigs
⅛ cup curly leaf parsley, finely chopped
⅛ cup yellow onion, ⅛-inch dice
⅛ cup celery, ⅛-inch dice
3 hardboiled eggs, finely chopped
Kosher salt, to taste
Finely ground black pepper, to taste

Preheat the oven to 350 degrees F.

Wash the potatoes under cool running water, and pat dry. Place them on a sheet tray, and bake for 70 to 90 minutes. Remove from the oven, place the potatoes in a kitchen towel one at a time, and gently remove and discard the skins while the potatoes are still warm. Refrigerate the potatoes for 2 hours, then cut them into 1-inch pieces, and place them in a large bowl.

In a separate bowl, mix the sour cream, mayonnaise, dill, parsley, onion, celery, and eggs, stirring until all the ingredients are well incorporated. Fold this mixture into the potatoes and season with salt and pepper to taste. Refrigerate, covered, for 4 to 6 hours before serving.

Our family has a couple of different recipes for potato salad that we like. This is one of the Dickey family favorites that we serve at the holidays.

LBJ Salad

When I first started making this salad at Dickey's decades ago, Lyndon Johnson had just finished his final term as president. One of our customers said that this salad should be called the LBJ salad because it had a red neck (I like to arrange the tomatoes in a circle around the bowl).

Serves 4 to 6

2 tomatoes, chopped
1 medium onion, peeled and chopped
1 medium cucumber, peeled and chopped
12 to 16 green olives, sliced
Salt, to taste
1 teaspoon black pepper
1 teaspoon white pepper
1 teaspoon garlic powder
2 tablespoons white vinegar
¼ cup olive oil

Mix the tomatoes, onion, cucumber, and olives together and set aside.

Make the marinade by whisking together the salt, black and white pepper, garlic, vinegar, and oil. Pour over the salad, toss, and refrigerate for 1 to 2 hours before serving.

Note: This salad will keep, refrigerated, for several days. It goes great with barbecue and other hearty meats.

Arugula Salad with Apple Dijon Dressing

Serves 4 to 6

Candied Pecans
1 cup sugar
1½ cups pecans, roughly chopped

Apple Dijon Dressing
4 cups apple juice
¼ cup apple cider vinegar
2 tablespoons shallot, grated
2 tablespoons Dijon mustard
1 tablespoon poppy seeds
1 cup olive oil
Salt and pepper, to taste

2 (5-ounce) bags fresh arugula
10 ounces goat cheese, crumbled, or feta cheese
½ pint yellow teardrop tomatoes

To make the candied pecans, cover a work surface with foil.

Stir the sugar and ¼ cup water into a medium saucepan over low heat until the sugar dissolves. Brush down the sides of the pan with a wet pastry brush. Increase the heat and boil without stirring, occasionally swirling the pan, for 9 minutes or until the mixture turns a deep amber color. Stir in the pecans and immediately pour the candied pecans out onto the foil, separating them with a fork. Allow the pecans to cool completely until the candy hardens. Set aside.

To make the salad dressing, boil the apple juice in a large, heavy saucepan for 20 minutes, or until the liquid has reduced to ½ cup. Transfer to a medium bowl, cover, and refrigerate until cold. Add the vinegar, shallots, Dijon mustard, and poppy seeds and gradually whisk in the olive oil. Season the dressing to taste with salt and pepper.

Toss the greens, cheese, tomatoes, and pecans in a salad bowl with enough dressing to coat, and serve.

Broccoli Salad

Serves 4 to 6

2 cups broccoli florets, washed and cut into bite-size pieces
2 cups cauliflower florets, washed and cut into bite-size pieces
½ cup carrots, peeled and sliced into ⅛-inch coins

Dressing
⅛ cup buttermilk ranch dressing, from your grocery
½ cup sour cream
2 tablespoons Miracle Whip mayonnaise
1 teaspoon sugar
1 teaspoon tarragon leaves, roughly chopped
1 tablespoon half-and-half
Garlic salt, to taste
Black pepper, to taste
5 yellow teardrop tomatoes, halved
5 red teardrop tomatoes, halved

Place the broccoli, cauliflower, and carrots in a bowl and gently toss.

To make the dressing, combine all of the ingredients except the garlic salt and black pepper and whisk until all the ingredients are well incorporated. Season to taste with the garlic salt and black pepper.

Add the dressing to the bowl of veggies and lightly toss using a spatula. Adjust the seasoning as desired. Garnish with the tomato halves and serve.

Caprese Salad

This is a great appetizer salad that my wife, Big Momma, loves. If you want to make it into a one-dish summer meal, you could top it with pickled shrimp.

Serves 4 to 6

2 or 3 large red or yellow tomatoes
8 to 10 ounces fresh mozzarella cheese
1 red onion
Olive oil, to coat
Coarse ground black pepper, to taste
Fresh basil, chopped, for garnish
Pickled shrimp, (recipe, p. 20)

Slice the tomatoes, cheese, and onion and arrange on a plate or platter. Drizzle the olive oil over the vegetables, then sprinkle the top with black pepper and chopped basil leaves. Store in the refrigerator until it is ready to be served. I know purists say not to refrigerate tomatoes, but this dish, to me, tastes better cold.

Before I go any further, I want to say a few things about this great country of ours. I believe in buying products made in America and that, of course, includes food. A great many non-American foods are available at grocery stores. But I always try to buy Gulf of Mexico shrimp, crawfish from Louisiana or catfish that come straight from the ponds of the good old U.S. of A. American-made food products are always better tasting and of higher quality than foreign competitors. Besides, I think buying American is the way to go.

Cucumber Salad

Serves 4 to 6

3 cups hothouse cucumbers
½ cup yellow onions, peeled and sliced ⅛-inch julienne
4 large tomatoes, chopped
2 teaspoons curly leaf parsley, stemmed and finely chopped

Dressing
⅓ cup Italian salad dressing, your favorite
⅓ cup honey mustard
2 teaspoons light brown sugar
¼ teaspoon black pepper

Cut the cucumbers in half lengthwise, slice them into ⅛-inch half-coins, and place them in a large bowl. Add the julienned onions and the tomato wedges. Add the chopped parsley.

In a separate bowl, whisk together the Italian salad dressing, mustard, brown sugar, and black pepper until all the ingredients are incorporated. Season to taste.

Pour the dressing over the vegetables and lightly toss using a spatula.

Ranch Cole Slaw

Serves 4 to 6

2½ cups (1 large) green cabbage, cored, quartered, and shredded
½ cup carrots, peeled and shredded
¼ cup red peppers, ⅛-inch dice

Dressing
¼ cup Miracle Whip mayonnaise
¼ cup regular mayonnaise
2 tablespoons sugar
2 tablespoons apple cider vinegar
White pepper, to taste

Place the shredded cabbage in a large bowl. Shred the peeled carrots using a cheese grater on the medium setting. Mix the cabbage, carrots, and red peppers together, tossing lightly with your hands. Set aside.

If you are not going to serve the slaw right away, cover the bowl with a damp paper towel and refrigerate. To make the dressing, add all the ingredients to a separate bowl and mix well. Pour the dressing over the cabbage mixture, and toss lightly. Chill before serving.

Blue Cheese Dressing

This recipe can be made in a couple of minutes. I guarantee ya your family will throw away any bottle of store-bought blue cheese dressing after they taste this. Steak houses serve it just like this over tomatoes and onions, as well as over any mixed green salad.

Yields 12 ounces

½ cup mayonnaise
½ cup buttermilk
½ cup blue cheese crumbles
6 twists black pepper

Combine the mayonnaise, buttermilk, and blue cheese in a bowl and stir with a fork until well mixed. Add 6 twists of black pepper from a peppermill and stir. Store in a covered plastic container and refrigerate until ready to serve. The dressing will keep for a couple days in the fridge as long as it is covered.

Note: Salad dressings should always be stored in a plastic container or plastic bag in the refrigerator. Using a metal container sometimes results in a metallic taste.

Thousand Island Dressing

Yields a little more than ½ cup

½ cup mayonnaise
3 tablespoons chili sauce (Hines preferred), or ketchup
1 teaspoon Louisiana hot sauce
6 twists black pepper
2 tablespoons sweet relish

Combine all the ingredients together in a bowl and stir. Cover and refrigerate until ready to use.

Note: If you can't find chili sauce, ketchup may be substituted. If you want the dressing to have a sweeter taste or to have more of a red color, just add more chili sauce or ketchup.

Your family will love this old-fashioned recipe. A lot of my friends like to add their own ingredients to the dressing, like chopped hard-boiled eggs or chopped green onions. These are great additions, but they are not necessary. This recipe is delicious on a salad or as a dip for shrimp.

Six Magic Words

Quite often Dickey's prepares barbecues for visiting government officials and wealthy business folks in the Dallas area. I can't help but laugh when I recall one story involving a prominent businessman with whom we were conducting business.

This particular individual, who was in the oil business, was pitching a drilling concession in Africa and wanted to host a barbecue for 15 or 16 of his potential clients. He was an important customer and requested our barbecue ribs and tenderloins. I personally handpicked some of my best employees for this assignment. Normally we set a 50-person minimum, but we waived the limit since he

was a regular customer. I wasn't planning to attend because I had promised my wife that I would take her out that night and I was confident that my capable staff could handle the event.

A couple of days before the barbecue, my phone rang. On the other end was the wealthy businessman who was hosting the event. Most big shots might ask their secretaries or assistants to call, but not him. He said, "Roland, I want you to come and smoke these tenderloins. I won't be happy unless you're there. Everything has to be perfect because we are on the verge of getting this drilling concession."

His request put me in a pickle. I had already promised my wife that we would go out that same night. I guess I hesitated because what he told me next certainly caught my attention. He said, "Roland I want to tell you six magic words that I think will change your mind. They are 'I don't care what it costs.'"

Needless to say, when I heard those magic words, I told my wife that she and I would have to re-schedule our date. My only question to the oil man was what time did he want me on the job.

As we say in the restaurant business: "No matter how big the company may get, it must revolve around the customers' needs."

DICKEY'S BARBECUE
Since ★ 1941

HOWDY

neighbor

FOOT-STOMPIN'
BARBECUE
AND RUBS

Rib-Ticklin' Rib Rub

Yields about 2 cups

½ cup salt
1 cup sugar
¼ cup paprika
1½ tablespoons granulated garlic
½ tablespoon ground cumin
1½ tablespoons lemon pepper

Thoroughly combine all the ingredients. You can store this rub in an airtight container for up to three months.

Old Recipe Barbecue Rub

This rub is great for ribs, pork, turkey, chicken, shrimp boil, crawfish, potatoes, and corn. Because it keeps for up to three months, I like to make it at the beginning of the summer and use it through the grilling season.

Yields about 8 cups

3 cups Rib Rub
¾ cups Grill Spice (see recipe, p. 49)
1½ cups ground cumin
1 teaspoon cayenne pepper
½ cup Lowery's Seasoning Salt
1¾ cups light brown sugar

Thoroughly combine all the ingredients, making sure the brown sugar lumps are broken up. You can store this rub in an airtight container for up to three months.

Grill Spice

Yields ½ cup

2 tablespoons granulated garlic
1 tablespoon sugar
1 tablespoon black pepper
2 tablespoons ground cumin
4 tablespoons sea salt

Mix all the ingredients together. Grill Spice may be kept stored in an airtight container for up to two weeks.

You can use this all-purpose rub on French Fries, hamburgers, egg dishes, or as a dry rub for meat.

Steak Rub

Yields ¼ cup

2 tablespoons ground coffee (whatever brand you like)
2 tablespoons Cajun seasoning
1 tablespoon salt

Combine all the dry ingredients together and rub on both sides of the steaks. Allow the steaks to sit out at least 1 hour to come to room temperature. This also gives the rub a chance to permeate the meat. Cook the steaks over a charcoal fire for 3 to 4 minutes per side for a medium-rare steak.

I invented this rub for Big Momma. She loves her steak rubbed with this and then grilled blood rare. These are great cooked outside over charcoal or inside under the broiler. You're going to be surprised at the subtle coffee taste, but believe me you will like it.

Hot 'N Spicy Barbecue Sauce

Yields 20 ounces

1 (19-ounce) bottle Dickey's Barbecue Sauce
1 teaspoon crushed red pepper flake
½ teaspoon granulated garlic

Mix all the ingredients together and refrigerate. This sauce will keep, refrigerated, for up to three days.

Sweet Barbecue Sauce

This is an excellent glaze for ribs and chicken that we developed for our stores in the South. We love a good sweet sauce on ribs.

Yields 20 ounces

1 (19-ounce) bottle Dickey's Barbecue Sauce
½ cup maple syrup

Add the maple syrup to the barbecue sauce and stir until combined. This sauce can be refrigerated and kept for up to three days.

Peppered Bacon Gravy

Yields 3 cups

⅓ cup bacon, ¼-inch dice
¼ cup (½ stick) unsalted butter
5 tablespoons all-purpose flour
2½ cups whole milk
1 teaspoon kosher salt
4 teaspoons cracked black pepper

Cook the bacon pieces in a medium stockpot over low heat for 8 to 9 minutes, stirring continuously. The bacon will render about ¼ cup of bacon fat.

When the bacon is rendered, add the butter and continue to cook. When the butter melts, whisk in the flour and continue to stir until it becomes a light tan color. Add in the milk very slowly, whisking in only 1 tablespoon at a time to prevent clumping.

Season the gravy with salt and pepper, and simmer for 8 to 10 minutes. Serve hot over grits, eggs, or biscuits.

Hickory Smoked Brisket

This brisket is wonderful served with gravy or mayonnaise on crusty French bread, like a real New Orleans Po' Boy! Save the leftovers for roast beef hash.

Serves 8 to 10
Smoking Temperature: 225 to 250 degrees F
Smoking Time: 45 to 60 minutes per pound
Kindling: Hickory log, quartered

One (4 to 6 pound) beef brisket
¼ cup Rib-Ticklin' Rib Rub (see recipe, p. 46)
3 tablespoons canola oil

Place some kindling and a few pieces of newspaper sprinkled with canola oil inside your firebox and light it. Once the fire burns steadily (in about 3 to 4 minutes) add a hickory log. Bring the temperature inside your smoker to between 225 and 250 degrees F. (Make sure your thermometer is calibrated correctly.)

Trim the fat cap on the top portion of the brisket if needed, allowing a ¼- to ½-inch thick cap to remain on the brisket.

Mix the barbecue rub with the canola oil. It should have the consistency of wet sand. Rub the entire brisket with the rub—front, sides, in all the cracks and crevices. Place the brisket fat-side up on the smoker. Place a foil loaf pan full of water as close to the firebox as possible and replenish the water as needed.

Maintaining a temperature between 225 and 250 degrees F, smoke the brisket for 8 to 9 hours (45 to 60 minutes per pound). You will need to check your temperature, adjust the vent, or replenish the wood, every 20 minutes during the smoking time.

Do not flip, turn, or poke the brisket with a fork at any time during this smoking process. When an instant thermometer reads between 190 and 200 degrees F, the beef is done. At Dickey's we perform what's called a "fork test." We place a meat fork in the fatty end (the deckle) of the brisket, and gently turn. If the meat is done, it should turn without resistance.

Place the brisket on a chopping block, and let it rest for 15 to 25 minutes. Slice against the grain, and serve.

Things you can do to pass the time while the brisket is smoking:

- *Read Lonesome Dove*
- *Polish your entire gun collection*
- *Learn to play at least ten Willie Nelson songs on the guitar*
- *Make a beer can pyramid*

A PRESIDENTIAL BARBECUE

Way back in 1975 I made it a priority to go to every single one of Dickey's catering jobs. We were building up the business and all our hard work paid off. We later became the biggest barbecue caterer in Dallas.

The following year our Republican congressman asked us to cater a barbecue for a Presidential candidate—a former actor by the name of Ronald Reagan who had served as governor of California. Reagan wanted to be the Republican nominee at the 1976 convention in Kansas City. (Of course, Reagan was unsuccessful that year but ended up snagging the 1980 nomination.)

The congressman asked us to put on a typical Texas barbecue for Reagan so the former governor could meet and greet some of the most successful oilmen and businessmen in Texas. The plan was to recruit the Texas men to become givers and fundraisers for Governor Reagan's 1976 campaign and others on down the road. I knew from the get-go that these fellows were going to be a tough sell and that they weren't going to be easily impressed. They were in their 50s and 60s, and all were sophisticated politicians who mostly had made money the hard way—they earned it.

The Reagan barbecue turned out to be unlike any other I had ever seen. When the former governor arrived, he strolled in wearing his characteristic charm and charisma right on his sleeve. His magnetic personality was something I had never seen before or since. It was electrifying. Believe me when I say I'm a veteran of countless barbecues as well as countless other functions where celebrities mingle with guests. Watching Reagan interact with the men was simply amazing. The businessmen wanted to touch Reagan's hand, his sleeve, or pat him on the back or shoulder. It was like Reagan was emitting special powers that they wanted to acquire.

These were guys who normally wouldn't give the time of day to a movie actor or celebrity. I knew right then and there that if Reagan were ever nominated for either party he would win. He had a certain something that I have never seen before in a politician.

Needless to say, the barbecue went great and Reagan was absolutely fantastic. He insisted on greeting all of our employees and being introduced to each and every one. The politicians and businessman who attended were impressed to no end by Reagan. Prior to meeting the charismatic Reagan, the men might have insisted they were lifelong Democrats. I'm not so sure they would have admitted that after schmoozing with the man who would become President.

Smoked Brisket Queso

Serves 4 to 6

1 (16-ounce) block Velveeta cheese, cut into ½-inch cubes
5 ounces tomatoes, seeded, ¼-inch dice
6 ounces canned green chilies, drained
4 ounces Dickey's chopped brisket, (recipe, p.52)
Milk, as needed
Cracked Black Pepper, to taste
1 large bag thick tortilla chips
1 teaspoon Dickey's Grill Spice, (recipe, p. 49)

Mix the cheese, tomatoes, green chilies, and chopped brisket, and place in a crockpot on medium heat. Stir every 3 to 5 minutes until the cheese melts completely. If the consistency is too thick, add a little milk and stir until heated through. Serve with thick tortilla chips dusted with Grill Spice (recipe, p. 49).

This is a great way to use leftover brisket. It also works well using the oven-baked brisket from my recipe on page 78.

Smoked Ham

Purchasing a cured ham will not only provide total ease of preparation, but will yield a fantastic flavor—plus it will take on the hickory smoke flavor incredibly well. Don't be afraid to cook a little extra. You can dice up the leftovers to add to your green beans.

Yields 3 to 4 pounds
Smoking Temperature: 270 to 295 degrees F
Smoking Time: 1½ to 2 hours
Kindling: Hickory log, quartered

**1 (6 to 8-pound) Mickleburry cured ham,
or other high-grade cured ham**

Place some kindling and a few pieces of newspaper sprinkled with canola oil inside the firebox of your smoker and light it. Once the fire burns steadily (in about 3 to 4 minutes), add a hickory log. Bring the temperature inside your smoker to between 270 and 295 degrees F. (Make sure your thermometer is calibrated.)

Place a foil loaf pan full of water as close to the firebox as possible and replenish the water as needed. Place the cured ham skin-side up inside the smoker. You will need to check your temperature, adjust the vent, or replenish the wood, every 20 minutes during the smoking time.

While maintaining a temperature between 270 and 295 degrees F, smoke the ham for 1 ½ to 2 hours, or until the skin of the ham is a burgundy color and an instant-read thermometer placed in the thickest part of the ham reads 160 degrees F.

Texas Smoked Hot Links

Serves 4 to 6
Smoking Temperature: 270 to 295 degrees F
Smoking Time: 25 to 30 minutes
Kindling: Hickory log, quartered

2 pounds Dickey's Texas Hot Link Sausage, or a good spicy sausage link
1 can beer, optional

Place some kindling and a few pieces of newspaper sprinkled with canola oil inside your firebox and light it. Once the fire burns steadily (in about 3 to 4 minutes) add a hickory log. Bring the temperature inside your smoker to between 270 and 295 degrees F. (Make sure your thermometer is calibrated.)

Place a foil loaf pan full of water as close to the firebox as possible and replenish the water as needed. You may substitute the can of beer for the water if you want to give the links a nice juicy flavor. You will need to check your temperature, adjust the vent, or replenish the wood, every 20 minutes during the smoking time.

Place the sausage links inside the smoker. While maintaining a temperature between 270 and 295 degrees F, smoke the sausage for 25 to 30 minutes, or until a toothpick inserted into the sausage loop causes the skin to "pop."

When the sausage is cooked, remove it from the smoker and allow it to rest for 3 to 5 minutes before slicing.

The secret to great smoked sausage is "snappy skins," which are achieved when the smoke tightens the casing around the meat.

Hickory Smoked Turkey

Serves 8 to 10
Smoking Temperature: 275 degrees F
Smoking Time: 35 minutes per pound
Kindling: Hickory chips

1 (12-pound) whole turkey, neck and giblets removed
1 small orange
12 to 15 whole cloves
1 bunch green kale, for garnish

Place the hickory chips into a pan, cover with water, and set aside.

Light the smoker and wait for the temperature of the smoker to come to 275 degrees F and the coals to burn to a white color.

Rinse the turkey under cold water, and pat dry.

Lightly oil the grate with vegetable oil or vegetable oil spray. (Do not spray the vegetable oil directly onto a grate over an open flame.)

Place the turkey onto the oiled grate. Add 2 handfuls of the damp chips to the smoker at the start of cooking, then add a handful every couple of hours during the cooking process.

Leave the lid closed during the smoking process, or you will let the heat out. Continue smoking until the internal temperature of the turkey reaches 180 degrees F. You may need to add charcoal briquettes to the fire in order to maintain the temperature in the smoker.

Serve the turkey whole on a platter lined with leafy greens. Stud an orange with the whole cloves and place it into the cavity of the turkey before serving.

Smoked Turkey Breast

Serves 4 to 6
Smoking Temperature: 270 to 295 degrees F
Smoking Time: 1½ to 2 hours
Kindling: Hickory log, quartered

2 to 3 pounds turkey breasts, skin on
Canola oil

Place some kindling and a few pieces of newspaper sprinkled with canola oil inside your firebox and light it. Once the fire burns steadily (in about 3 to 4 minutes) add a hickory log. Bring the temperature inside your smoker to between 270 and 295 degrees F. (Make sure your thermometer is calibrated.)

Place a foil loaf pan full of water as close to the firebox as possible and replenish the water as needed. You will need to check your temperature, adjust the vent, or replenish the wood, every 20 minutes during the smoking time. Place the turkey breasts skin-side up inside the smoker.

While maintaining a temperature between 270 and 295 degrees F, smoke the turkey for 1 ½ to 2 hours, or until the skin is golden brown in color and an instant-read thermometer placed in the thickest part of the breast reads 160 degrees F.

Tips for Tasty Turkeys

Typically at Thanksgiving and Christmas we serve a tenderloin or prime rib. Our family likes turkeys but we aren't turkey lovers, except for my wife Maurine, who sometimes thinks I'm a turkey. However, a lot of our great customers can't get enough turkey and we do everything we can to please those who like smoked turkey.

Back when I lived at home with my parents, my mother did all she could to keep the turkey breast from drying out. She put tin foil over it, and moistened parchment cloth to cover the breast—all to no avail. Her initial techniques helped, but the turkeys still didn't turn out as juicy as she wanted. Finally, she toothpicked four or five strips of raw bacon to the breast of the turkey before cooking it. She worked magic with those toothpicks and bacon!

She basted the bacon-covered turkey breast and turned on the broiler just a few minutes to brown it. Remember, most people prefer white meat, so that's what you have to keep moist during cooking. Folks might take a bite or two out of a turkey leg, but, other than that, nobody seems to want the rest of the bird. That's why I prefer cooking a turkey breast if I am going to cook a turkey at all.

The best reason to cook the whole turkey is for its appearance on your holiday table.

Sweet-Glazed Barbecue Chicken

Serves 4
Smoking Temperature: 270 to 295 degrees F
Smoking Time: 2½ to 3 hours
Kindling: Hickory log, quartered

1 whole chicken, halved
4 tablespoons Rib Ticklin' Rib Rub (recipe, p.46)
Dickey's Sweet Barbecue Sauce, as desired, (recipe, p.50)

The day before you want to barbecue, wash the chicken under cold water, remove any loose parts, and pat dry with a paper towel. Cut the chicken in half using a pair of kitchen shears. Cut down both sides of the backbone and remove the bone and discard it. Then cut down the center of the breast to halve the chicken. Rub 2 tablespoons of Dickey's Rib Rub over the entire chicken half. Cover and refrigerate for 24 hours.

The next day, place some kindling and a few pieces of newspaper sprinkled with canola oil inside your firebox and light. Once the flame burns steadily (in about 3 to 4 minutes) add a hickory log and bring the temperature inside your smoker to between 270 and 295 degrees F. (Make sure your thermometer is calibrated.)

Place a foil loaf pan full of water in the smoker as close to the firebox as possible. Replenish the water in the pan as needed. Place the chicken halves skin-side up on a rack inside the smoker.

Allow the chicken halves to smoke for 2 ½ to 3 hours, or until the chicken is a golden brown color and the skin is lightly crispy. An instant-read thermometer placed in the chicken should read 175 degrees F.

You will need to check your temperature, adjust the vent, or replenish the wood every 20 minutes during the smoking time.

Glaze the chicken with Dickey's Sweet Barbecue Sauce and let it rest for 3 to 5 minutes before serving.

Polish-Style Sausage

Serves 8 to 10
Smoking Temperature: 270 to 295 degrees F
Smoking Time: 25 to 30 minutes
Kindling: Hickory log, quartered

2 loops (2 pounds) Polish-style sausage

Place some kindling and a few pieces of newspaper sprinkled with canola oil inside your firebox and light. Once the kindling is burning steadily (in about 3 to 4 minutes), add a hickory log, quartered.

Bring the temperature inside your smoker between 270 and 295 degrees F. (Make sure your thermometer is calibrated.) Place the sausage loops inside the smoker, and place a foil loaf pan full of water as close to the firebox as possible.

Replenish the water as needed. While maintaining a temperature between 270 and 295 degrees F, smoke the sausage for 25 to 30 minutes. Be sure to check the temperature, adjust the vent, and replenish the wood as needed, every 10 or so minutes during this time.

The secret to great smoked sausage is a "snappy skin," which is achieved when the smoke tightens the casing around the meat. To test for this, use a toothpick and give the sausage loop a quick prick. If you feel a "pop" then you know it is perfect.

Remove the sausage from the smoker and let it rest for 3 to 5 minutes before slicing.

Hickory Smoked Pulled Pork

Serves 10 to 12
Smoking Temperature: 225 to 250 degrees F
Smoking Time: 45 to 60 minutes per pound
Kindling: Hickory log, quartered

1 (4 to 6-pound) pork butt, bone-in
3 ounces Rib Ticklin' Rib Rub (see recipe, p. 46)

Place the pork butt on a clean sheet tray, and allow it come to room temperature.

Place some kindling and a few pieces of newspaper sprinkled with canola oil inside the firebox in your smoker and light it. Once the fire burns steadily (in about 3 to 4 minutes), add a hickory log. Bring the temperature inside your smoker to between 225 and 250 degrees F. (Make sure your thermometer is calibrated correctly.)

Place the pork butt fat-side up in the center of a piece of foil that is 1 ½ foot square. Sprinkle Dickey's Rib Rub over the entire pork butt and rub it in with your hands. Fold up the sides of the foil to make a bowl, and place the pork butt on the smoker.

Place a foil loaf pan full of water in the smoker as close to the firebox as possible. Replenish the water in the pan as needed.

While maintaining a temperature between 225 and 250 degrees F, smoke the pork for 8 to 9 hours (45 to 60 minutes per pound).

You will need to check your temperature, adjust the vent, or replenish the wood, every 20 minutes during the smoking time.

Do not flip, turn, or poke the pork with a fork at any time during this smoking process. When a thermometer reads between 190 and 200 degrees F, the pork is done. At Dickey's we perform what's called a "fork test." Place a meat fork in the top part of the pork butt and turn it gently. If the meat is done, it should turn without resistance.

Place the smoked pork on a chopping block, and let it rest for 15 to 25 minutes before you pull it. Do not forget, as you "pull" you will need to remove the bone from the center of the pork. I don't use knives of any sort for pulled pork. I use a Dickey's specialized technique called the "Grab, Squish and Tickle!"

Technical Terms for Pulling Pork

GRAB: With your hands, GRAB a portion of the pork

SQUISH: With your palms, SQUISH it to separate the strands

TICKLE: With your fingers, TICKLE the strands to create that signature "pulled" look

Pork Ribs with Sweet Barbecue Sauce

Yields one rack (11 to 13 ribs)
Smoking Temperature: 270 to 295 degrees F
Smoking Time: 3 to 3½ hours
Kindling: Hickory log, quartered

1 rack St. Louis-style pork ribs
3 ounces Rib Ticklin' Rib Rub (see recipe, p.46)
Sweet Barbecue Sauce, as desired (see recipe, p. 50)

Place some kindling and a few pieces of newspaper sprinkled with canola oil inside your firebox and light. Once the flame burns steadily (in about 3 to 4 minutes) add a hickory log and bring the temperature inside your smoker to between 270 and 295 degrees F. (Make sure your thermometer is calibrated.)

Sprinkle Dickey's Rib Rub over the entire rib rack and use your hands to rub it in. Place the ribs bone-side down on the smoker. This will allow the smoke to channel under the ribs and achieve an overall smoked flavor.

Place a foil loaf pan full of water in the smoker as close to the firebox as possible. Replenish the water in the pan as needed.

While maintaining a temperature between 270 and 295 degrees F, smoke the pork ribs for 3 to 3 1/2 hours. Be sure to check your temperature, adjust the vent, or replenish the wood every 20 minutes during the smoking time. Do not flip, turn, or poke the ribs with a fork at any time during this process.

I suggest performing what's called a "break test" for doneness. Grab the rib rack with a pair of tongs. If they immediately begin to "break," (not bounce) they're ready. If they are still "bouncy" let them smoke for another 20 minutes. Once all the ribs have passed the "break test," remove them from the smoker, set aside and let them rest for 5 to 7 minutes.

To cut and serve, flip the ribs bone-side up to get a cleaner cut and allow the bones to be more visible. Make a clean cut between the bones. You should get 11 to 13 ribs from one rack. Flip the ribs over and glaze them with Dickey's Sweet Barbecue Sauce and serve hot.

What in the world do you do with leftovers?

I must admit that I absolutely, positively despised leftovers when I was growing up. And I know why. My mom would serve roast beef one day and for the next couple of days, she'd set out that same old, tired roast beef on the table. For Pete's Sake, if you're going to eat leftovers, change them. Jazzing them up isn't that difficult and the hungry folks sitting at your table will be glad you did.

I love a good roasted turkey and when I do cook one, I like serving it with all the trimmings. Usually we have plenty of leftover turkey, which means in the days to come I can fix myself and Big Momma a treat that we call the Hot Brown Sandwich. The original sandwich has roots in Kentucky and has a cream sauce instead of the cheese sauce that we like. I've never met a kid or a hungry husband who didn't want something covered in a melted cheese sauce.

Here's how we do it: Place a few slices of toasted bread or buns in an oven-proof dish. Add a layer of turkey followed by slices of Swiss or cheddar cheese. Cover with cheese sauce, top with a slice of Swiss cheese, and broil in the oven until the Swiss cheese begins to melt.

Another favorite leftover transformation is something I call Beef and Wine (recipe, p. 99).

Here are a few more tips to spruce up leftovers:

★ Dice up a little leftover brisket and toss it in a potful of green beans.

★ Have leftover sausage? Whip up an omelet with a kick (recipe for Leftover Sausage Omelet, p. 140)

★ Too much pork? Add pasta and a few favorite ingredients for a different take on the usual pasta (recipe, p. 69).

Leftover Barbecue Pork Pasta

Serves 4

2 tablespoons olive oil
1 cup chopped onions
1 pound chopped leftover pork
1 teaspoon garlic powder
4 to 6 ounces Dickey's barbecue sauce
½ pound dried pasta
½ cup grated Parmesan, Swiss or cheddar cheese, for garnish

Sauté the onions in olive oil in a skillet over medium heat for 2 minutes, or until soft, then add the chopped pork. Continue cooking for 2 to 3 minutes, then add the garlic powder and barbecue sauce. Mix well and heat until piping hot.

Cook the pasta separately in boiling water according to the package directions. Drain and pour the pasta into a mixing bowl, then top with the sauce and pork mixture.

Top the pasta with Parmesan cheese—or grated Swiss or cheddar if you prefer—and serve.

This is a great way to use leftovers. Pork has enough built-in fat (but not too much) to make it re-heatable without drying out the meat. Kids love this dish.

Stuffed Pork Chops

Pork chops were once known as 'Poor Man's Steak.' Pork is a dense meat and can taste dry, so you must know how to prepare the chops to keep them juicy. These are wonderful served with steamed rice. Don't be surprised if everyone wants more chops!

Serves 4
Cooking Time: 35 to 45 minutes

4 (1-inch thick) pork chops, bone-in
Salt, to taste
Pepper, to taste
2 tablespoons extra virgin olive oil
3 cloves garlic, chopped
1 cup chopped onions
½ cup white wine
2½ cups chicken stock
2 bay leaves

Rub the chops with salt and pepper and set aside. Heat the olive oil in a skillet and brown the chops over medium heat for 30 seconds on each side. Use tongs to remove the chops from the skillet. Drain off any excess fat.

In the same skillet, sauté the garlic and onions for 2 minutes. Add in the white wine and chicken stock to deglaze the pan, scraping up the meat bits. Add the bay leaves and salt and pepper to taste. Cook for 3 to 4 more minutes, or until the liquid has reduced a little, before returning the chops to the pan. Lower the heat to a simmer and cook the chops for 35 to 45 minutes, or until the meat falls off the bone. There should be no knife required to eat these chops!

Texas Mussels Mariners

Serves 4 to 6
Cook Time: 15 minute

2 pounds cultivated mussels, scrubbed
2 tablespoons (¼ stick) unsalted butter
½ shallot, chopped
2 cloves garlic, thinly sliced
1 cup Chardonnay or dry white wine
3 tablespoons heavy cream
2 tablespoons Dickeys Old Recipe Barbecue Rub, (recipe, p. 46)

Garnish
Chopped parsley
Dickey's Grill Spice, optional, (recipe, p. 49)

Rinse and clean the mussels, rejecting any broken or open shells. In a large, high-sided sauté pan over medium-high heat, heat the butter until softened, and add the shallot and garlic. Sauté for 2 minutes, or until the garlic has caramelized.

Deglaze the pan with the white wine for 1 minute, allowing the wine to come to a simmer. Once the wine is simmering, add the mussels to the pan. Cook for 6 to 8 minutes, or until all the shells have opened. Discard the mussels that are still closed. Remove the shallots from the saucepan, place them in a bowl, and set aside. Put the mussels in a separate dish.

Increase the heat under the saucepan to high, add the cream, and whisk for 30 seconds. Remove the pan from the heat, sprinkle with chopped parsley and Dickey's Grill Spice if you want to add heat. Pour over the mussels and serve hot.

I know people that like to use the French word for mussels, "moules," but I want to call them by the American name, mussels. Calling them "moules" just doesn't stick with me.

Beef Tacos

You can either use cooked ground beef or leftover beef brisket for this recipe—I even like to use leftover pulled pork sometimes. It's good eatin' either way. This is a great meal not only for the kids, but for adults, too.

Yields 8 to 10 tacos

1 pound ground beef, or leftover beef or pork brisket
2 to 3 tablespoons salsa, plus more for serving
1 onion, chopped
1 head lettuce, chopped
2 tomatoes, chopped
10 hard taco shells (*I like the ones that look like they came from Taco Bell*)
1 cup grated cheddar cheese

Cook the ground beef in a sauté pan until brown, then drain off any excess fat. (If you're using leftovers, heat the leftovers in a sauté pan over medium heat until it's warm enough to serve.) Stir in 2 to 3 tablespoons of salsa, either hot or mild. Place the meat in a serving bowl and set aside.

Place the chopped onions, lettuce, tomatoes, salsa, and cheese in individual bowls. I like to prepare a "taco bar" where everyone can build their own tacos. Lay all of these ingredients out buffet-style on the kitchen counter or dining table and allow guests to serve themselves. Be sure to have plenty of extra ingredients.

Whole Tenderloin

Serves 8 to 10

1 whole beef tenderloin
¼ cup extra virgin olive oil, plus more for blue cheese mixture
Sea salt, to taste
Coarse black pepper, to taste
4 to 6 ounces crumbled blue cheese
⅔ cup chopped pecans

Preheat the oven to 375 degrees F.

Rub the outside of the tenderloin with olive oil, salt, and pepper. Make a 1-inch-deep pocket down the center of the tenderloin and set aside.

In a small bowl, mix the blue cheese and chopped pecans with a little olive oil to make it stick together. Stuff the blue cheese mixture inside the pocket of the tenderloin. Place the tenderloin, stuffing-side up, on a large baking sheet and place in the oven. Cook for 35 minutes for rare, or 45 minutes for medium. Remove the tenderloin from the oven and allow to sit for 15 minutes before carving and serving.

For special occasions, there is nothing like a whole tenderloin. As an east Dallas boy, I realize that whole tenderloin can be expensive, but it's worth it. Be sure to buy an oven-prepared tenderloin trimmed of all fat and silver skin.

Baked Brisket

Dickeys sells millions of pounds of smoked brisket every year, so I like to occasionally bake a brisket (like your Grandmother used to do) for a different taste. Brisket can be tough unless it's cooked for a long time at a low temperature, like in this recipe.

Serves 8 to 10
Cooking Time: 7 to 8 hours

1 (6 to 7-pound) beef brisket
2 tablespoons coarse sea salt
1 teaspoon black pepper
2 ounces canned beef stock
2 ounces red wine
1 onion, sliced
2 cloves garlic, crushed
2 tablespoons Worcestershire sauce

Preheat the oven to 225 degrees F.

Rub the brisket thoroughly with salt and pepper, and use a knife to score the brisket in tic-tac-toe shaped squares so that the spices will better penetrate the meat. Place the brisket in a large roasting pan, fat-side up. Pour the stock, wine, onion, garlic, and Worcestershire sauce around the brisket. Cook, covered, for 7 to 8 hours. The meat should be fork tender when it is done. Transfer the brisket from the baking pan to a cutting board and allow it to sit and drain until the brisket reaches room temperature. Trim the fat and slice the brisket across the grain.

To serve with Au Jus, save the pan drippings and skim off as much fat as possible. Cook the drippings over medium heat until the liquid has reduced by half. This will concentrate the flavor of the gravy.

Make a different side sauce by mixing equal parts mayonnaise and sour cream, and adding store-bought horseradish to taste.

Leg of Lamb

Serves 4 to 6
Cooking Time: 6 to 8 hours

1 (5-pound) leg of lamb
4 ounces Dijon or Creole mustard
Sea salt, to taste
1 tablespoon coarse cracked pepper
¼ cup crushed dried mint
1 cup red wine
1 cup chopped onions
4 tablespoons Worcestershire sauce
2 bay leaves

Preheat the oven to 225 degrees F.

Rub the leg of lamb thoroughly with the mustard, salt, pepper, and mint. Place it in a roasting pan and cover with the wine, onions, Worcestershire sauce, bay leaves, and 1 cup water. Cover and cook for 6 to 8 hours, or until the meat is fork tender.

Remove the meat from the pan and allow the lamb to sit on a cutting board for 15 minutes before slicing. If you want to serve a sauce with this dish, reserve the pan drippings and skim off as much fat as possible. Keep the sauce warm in a separate skillet until you are ready to serve.

This recipe is very similar to one created by a great Cajun cook, Justin Wilson, who passed 10 years ago. I had the honor to meet him in the early '90s. My original recipe called for cooking this lamb dish until medium rare, but my family prefers it cooked to fork tender.

Shrimp-Stuffed Bell Peppers

This is the recipe for bell peppers that Big Momma likes best. My favorite is on the next page.

Serves 4

½ pound raw shrimp, peeled and deveined
3 cloves garlic
1 cup chopped celery
1 cup chopped onions
1 tablespoon olive oil
1 teaspoon cayenne pepper
1 teaspoon black pepper
1 tablespoon salt
1 tablespoon Louisiana hot sauce
1 cup bread crumbs
1 egg, beaten
Juice of 1 lemon
1 lemon, quartered
2 bell peppers, halved, cored, and seeded
1 (8-ounce) can tomato sauce
Butter, for serving

Preheat the oven to 350 degrees F.

Chop the shrimp into small pieces and set aside. Sauté the garlic, celery, and onions in olive oil for 3 to 4 minutes, then transfer to a bowl. Add the cayenne pepper, black pepper, salt, and hot sauce to the bowl. Stir in the shrimp, bread crumbs, and beaten egg. If the mixture seems too dry, add olive oil to hold it together. Stuff the bell pepper halves with the shrimp mixture and place in a casserole dish.

In a small bowl, dilute the tomato sauce with ½ cup water, pour the sauce around the bell peppers and bake for 30 minutes. Remove the peppers from the oven and pour the lemon juice evenly over the peppers. Garnish with the lemon wedges and serve.

Note: If you are not worried about calories, then add a pat of butter to each pepper and bake for another 5 minutes.

Beef-Stuffed Bell Peppers

Serves 4
Cooking Time: 45 minutes

2 cloves garlic, chopped
1 cup chopped onions
½ cup chopped celery
2 tablespoons olive oil
1 tablespoon Louisiana hot sauce
1 teaspoon Worcestershire sauce
1 tablespoon ground pepper
1 tablespoon Louisiana seasoning salt
1 cup cooked white rice
½ pound ground sirloin
2 bell peppers, halved, cored, and seeded
1 (8-ounce) can tomato sauce

Preheat the oven to 350 degrees F.

Sauté the garlic, onion, and celery in the olive oil over medium heat for 3 to 4 minutes, or until soft. Set aside in a bowl and allow to cool. Once cool, add the hot sauce, Worcestershire sauce, pepper, and seasoning salt and mix well. Add the cooked rice and raw ground sirloin. Mix well, roll into 4 balls, and place into the 4 bell pepper halves. Shape the meat and rice mixture to fit in each of the hollowed bell pepper halves. Place the peppers into a casserole dish.

In a separate bowl, mix the tomato sauce with 1 cup water and pour around the peppers into the casserole. Cover with foil and bake for 45 minutes, or until the peppers are soft and the meat is well done.

Baked Chicken

Serves 4 to 6
Cooking Time: 50 minutes

8 chicken legs or thighs
½ cup mayonnaise
2 tablespoons Cajun seasoning (or a mixture of salt and pepper)

Preheat the oven to 375 degrees F.

Rub the chicken pieces all over with the Cajun seasoning, then rub the mayonnaise over the seasoning. Place the chicken on a broiler rack or in a glass pan and bake for 50 minutes, or until the skin is crispy, the chicken is tender, and juices run clear.

Big Momma likes chicken baked in the oven better than just about anything. We always buy pieces rather than a whole chicken because she and I both prefer dark meat; however, if you want to use a whole chicken for this recipe, it works fine. The mayonnaise makes the chicken skin crispy, but don't tell anyone if you're worried about calories. A lot of restaurants use this type of baking preparation for fish, but I have been using it for years with chicken and I never tell Big Momma how it gets so brown and crispy.

Texas "Nuff Said" Chili

To make a wonderful, slightly smoky version of this Texas chili, substitute 1 pound of chopped barbecue beef for the ground beef. To really spike it up, add an additional ½ pound of sausage and 1 can of ranch style beans.

Serves 8
Cooking Time: 2 hours and 15 minutes

2 pounds ground beef, coarse ground
1 (8-ounce) can tomato sauce
1 cup beef stock
1 cup Shiner Bock beer, or your favorite beer
2 fresh jalapeños, whole
3 tablespoons dark chili powder
2 tablespoons granulated onion
2 chicken bouillon cubes
½ teaspoon cayenne pepper
3 teaspoons smoked paprika
2 teaspoons granulated garlic
1 tablespoon ground cumin
2 teaspoons masa
Black pepper, finely ground, to taste
Kosher salt, to taste

Garnish
Shredded cheese
Whole or sliced jalapeños
Diced yellow onions

Cook the ground beef in a large pot over medium-low heat for 3 to 5 minutes. Do not allow the beef to brown. Drain the beef in a colander and return the beef to the pot. Add the tomato sauce, beef stock, Shiner Bock, and ¾ cup of water. Add the whole jalapeños, cover, and simmer over low heat for 40 minutes. Add water as needed.

Stir in the chili powder, granulated onion, and chicken bouillon cubes, stir, then cover and continue to simmer for 45 minutes more. Add water as needed. Stir in the cayenne, paprika, granulated garlic, and cumin.

Add a little water to the masa to make a loose paste and stir this into the simmering chili. Cover and simmer for another 40 minutes. Season to taste with pepper and salt, serve with corn bread (recipe, pg. 146) or crackers, and pass bowls of shredded cheese, jalapeños, and diced yellow onions for garnish.

Smothered Short Ribs

Serves 6

2 tablespoons olive oil
12 beef short ribs
½ cup chopped bell pepper
½ cup chopped celery
1 cup chopped onions
6 to 7 cloves garlic, peeled and sliced
4 ounces red wine
18 ounces beef stock
3 bay leaves
1 tablespoon Louisiana hot sauce
1 tablespoon Worcestershire sauce
Salt, to taste
Pepper, to taste

Beef short ribs are an inexpensive cut of meat that are delicious if cooked properly. If not, they can be as tough as a 35 cent steak. I like to serve the ribs with rice or a crusty French bread. I also serve bread and butter pickles and sliced onion on the side, along with some good red wine. This is a great meal and it's not expensive. Remember that beef ribs are a fatty product, so for those who don't want to meet any meat that has fat in it, this recipe is not for you.

Heat 1 tablespoon olive oil in a large skillet over medium heat. Add the ribs and cook for 3 to 4 minutes on each side, or until crispy. Remove the ribs and remove the excess fat from the skillet, replacing it with 1 tablespoon fresh olive oil.

Add the bell peppers, celery, onions, and garlic to the oil and sauté for 3 to 4 minutes, or until soft. Return the beef ribs to the skillet, add the wine, and continue to cook for 3 to 4 minutes, or until the alcohol burns off.

Add the stock, bay leaves, Louisiana hot sauce, Worcestershire sauce, salt, and pepper. Cover, lower the heat, and cook on a slow simmer for 1 ½ to 2 ½ hours, or until the meat falls off the bone. You can also cook this recipe in a covered stockpot in the oven at 300 degrees F for 3 to 3 ½ hours. When the ribs are tender, remove them from the heat. Serve the short ribs with their sauce on the side.

Pork Tenderloin

My wife likes to serve this with Dickey's barbecue sauce. If you don't care for barbecue sauce, this roast is so nice and juicy it really doesn't need anything else.

My problem with most roast pork recipes it is that they are always too dry. Remember, the pork we have today is much more lean and dense than it was 20 to 30 years ago.

I tried cooking a tenderloin covered, uncovered, barbecued—all to no avail. It always came out too dry because there is no fat to protect it. I finally overcame this by wrapping a well-seasoned pork tenderloin in raw bacon.

Serves 2 to 4
Cooking Time: 25 minutes

1 (1½-pound) boneless pork tenderloin
4 tablespoons Cajun seasoning, or
   Rib Ticklin' Rib Rub, (recipe, p. 46)
6 strips bacon

Preheat the oven to 400 degrees F.

Rub the tenderloin with the seasoning, then wrap it completely in bacon. Secure the bacon to the tenderloin with toothpicks if necessary. Place the tenderloin on a grill rack and place the rack inside a large 1½-inch-deep baking pan. Cook, uncovered, for 25 minutes if the roast is 1½ to 2 pounds, or until the bacon is crispy. If the roast is larger, cook for 25 minutes per pound. After 15 minutes, baste the roast with the bacon drippings from the pan.

Once the roast is done, remove it from the oven and allow it to sit for 20 minutes to cool. You can slice and serve the tenderloin with the bacon still on, or remove the bacon to slice and serve.

Grilled Shrimp

Serves 6
Cooking Time: 25 minutes

30 (5 shrimp per kabob) raw Gulf Mexican shrimp, cleaned and peeled
Juice of 3 lemons
1 teaspoon coarse salt
1 teaspoon fresh ground black pepper
1 teaspoon cayenne pepper (optional)
2 to 3 tablespoons olive oil

Marinate the shrimp in the refrigerator for 1 hour in the lemon juice, salt, both peppers and olive oil. After an hour, thread the shrimp onto the kabob skewers so they are close together, or they'll dry out very quickly while cooking.

Grill the shrimp kabobs over red hot coals for about 2 minutes, then turn and baste with the marinade. Cook for another minute, then turn the kabob over and cook for another 3 to 4 minutes. You'll know the shrimp are done when they are completely pink. If the middles are not turning pink, you can separate the shrimp a little on the skewers. Do not overcook shrimp or they'll become rubbery. Baste again with the marinade before removing them from the grill. Place them on a platter and serve hot.

If you want to stretch this recipe and serve it as an appetizer, make each kabob using only 2 shrimp per skewer. However you serve this, your guests are gonna love them!

Horseshoe Sandwich

The horseshoe sandwich was invented by Joe Schweska in 1928 at the Woodland Hotel in Springfield, Illinois. Joe was the chef at the Woodland Hotel in the late 1920s and the beginning of WW II, and he wanted to make something that was filling and wouldn't break the bank for the races, hence the name horseshoe sandwich. Originally it was made with hamburger patties, but I think it's great with other meats—especially leftovers. This is not a sandwich you will want if you are on a diet, and if you eat the whole thing you may feel like you've got a horseshoe in your stomach.

Serves 4

1 package frozen French fries, your favorite brand
1 pound cooked leftover roast, sliced, or other sandwich meat
1 loaf sandwich bread, sliced and toasted
Mayonnaise, as desired

Cheese Sauce
2 tablespoons (¼ stick) butter
6 ounces Velveeta Cheese
2 cups grated sharp cheddar cheese
¼ teaspoon dry mustard
1 teaspoon Worcestershire sauce
4 tablespoons whipping cream
1 teaspoon cayenne pepper (optional)

Cook the French fries in the oven according to the package directions, being sure to cook until the fries are crispy.

To make the cheese sauce, melt the butter in the top half of a double boiler, being careful not to let the water touch the top of the boiler. Add the Velveeta and cheddar cheese to the butter, and whisk together slowly. Add the mustard and stir until combined, then add the Worcestershire sauce. Whisk in the whipping cream last, and the cayenne if desired. Set aside while you assemble the sandwiches.

Note: This may seem like a lot of work for the sauce, but it's the cheese sauce that makes the sandwich. When I make this sauce for my sons, they ask me to add cayenne pepper to it to make it hot.

Take two pieces of bread side by side on a plate and cover one side of each slice with mayonnaise. Place the sliced meat on each slice of bread, and cover with a small amount of cheese sauce. Place a handful of fries on top, then cover with more cheese sauce and serve immediately.

Spaghetti a la Puttanesca

This is my son Cullen's recipe and one of our family's all-time favorite pasta dishes! It's a nice briny and spicy sauce with olives and capers. Spend the extra money to buy a premium dried pasta and be careful to serve it al dente (don't over-cook it!).

Serves 4
Cooking Time: 20 minutes

3 cloves garlic, minced
¼ cup extra virgin olive oil
1 tablespoon salt-packed capers, rinsed
1 cup brine-cured Kalamata olives, pitted and roughly chopped
1 (28-ounce) can tomato sauce
1 teaspoon dried red pepper flakes
⅓ teaspoon fresh ground black pepper
Kosher salt, to taste
1 pound dried spaghetti
2 tablespoons flat-leaf parsley, minced

Sauté the garlic in olive oil in a large saucepan over medium heat until it just starts to change color. Add the capers, olives, tomato sauce, and red and black pepper. Bring the sauce to a boil, then reduce the heat to low and simmer for 15 minutes. While the sauce is simmering, cook the spaghetti in a large stockpot with well salted boiling water, according to the cooking time on the package for al dente pasta.

Drain the pasta, reserving 2 cups of the cooking water in a separate bowl. Add the drained pasta to the sauce mixture, and increase the heat to high. Cook for 30 seconds, tossing constantly, using tongs to coat the pasta with the sauce mixture together in the pan. Add some of the reserved cooking water if the sauce is too thick to coat the pasta. Transfer the pasta to a large serving bowl, sprinkle with chopped fresh parsley and a splash of extra virgin olive oil, and serve immediately.

Big Roland's Favorite Pasta

Serves 1
Cooking Time: 10 minutes

1 bottle Chianti or Cabernet Sauvignon
⅓ pound pasta (angel hair, penne, or your favorite)
6 garlic cloves, crushed
3 ounces extra virgin olive oil
4 ounces fresh white mushrooms, sliced
3 slices bacon, cut into small cubes
1 egg, beaten
Grated Parmesan cheese, to taste
Salt and pepper, to taste

Open the red wine and enjoy a glass or two. Wine is for use in the recipe, but also to keep the cook happy!

Bring a large stockpot of water to a rolling boil, add the pasta, and cook for 7 minutes, or until the pasta is al dente. Drain the cooked pasta and set aside in a large bowl. In a sauté pan, cook the garlic in the olive oil for 2 minutes. Add the mushrooms and bacon and continue to cook for 3 or 4 more minutes, or until the mushrooms are tender. Add the olive oil and bacon mixture to the pasta. Stir in the egg, Parmesan cheese, and salt and pepper to taste.

Toss well and serve with another glass of red wine!

Note: Sometimes I will add extra olive oil to the pasta if it is too dry. Another great option is to stir ½ cup frozen peas into the hot pasta, or add a teaspoon of ground red pepper for some heat.

Big Momma isn't especially fond of pasta, so I make it for myself when she's out of town. That's the reason that the recipe serves just one.

Cuba Libre Holiday Ham

Save the ham bone to cook with butter beans or freeze for later use. I like to cut up the leftover ham and freeze the portions to use in lots of different dishes.

Serves 6 to 8
Cooking Time: 2 to 3 hours

1 (6 to 8-pound) ham, bone-in, uncooked
1 small jar Maraschino cherries, quartered
4 ounces rum (light or dark)
12 ounces real Coca-Cola
Juice of 2 limes
1 cup chicken broth
1 cup chopped onions

Before placing the ham in the oven, use a knife to make a tic-tac-toe pattern of ½-inch deep cuts across the fatty part of the ham. Embed the cherries in these slits all across the top of the ham. Place the ham in a roasting pan and add the rum, Coca-Cola, lime juice, broth, and onion around ham. Cover and bake at 350 degrees F for 2 hours. If you are using a larger ham, cook it for 3 hours, or until the ham is fork-tender. Remove from the oven and uncover, then place back in the oven for 45 minutes, or until brown.

Note: Before returning the ham to the oven, a lot of folks like to pour maple syrup over the top of the ham, giving it a sweet taste.

I like to serve this dish with actual Cuba Libres, made with rum, coke, and lime juice on ice.

Fried Catfish

Serves 4 to 6

1 egg
1½ cups whole milk
1½ cups yellow cornmeal
20 Ritz crackers, finely crushed
1 tablespoon kosher salt
1 tablespoon Tony Chachere's seasoning
2 teaspoons cayenne pepper
2 teaspoons smoked paprika
2 teaspoons coarse black pepper

Seasoning
2 tablespoons kosher salt
1½ tablespoons ground black pepper
1 teaspoon cayenne pepper

3 to 4 catfish filets, cut into strips
Canola oil, for frying

Preheat a fryer filled with enough canola oil to allow the fish to float and heat the oil to 360 degrees F. Whisk together the eggs and whole milk in a bowl, and set aside.

Using a separate bowl with deep sides, stir together the cornmeal, crackers, salt, Tony Chacere's seasoning, cayenne, paprika, and black pepper to make the dredging mix.

In a third bowl, mix together the salt, black pepper, and cayenne for the seasoning. Rinse the filets, pat them dry, and cut them into medium-sized strips.

Season the catfish strips liberally, then dip them in the egg wash and the seasoning again. Dredge the strips in the cornmeal mix and fry them in the hot oil for 7 to 8 minutes, turning, until they are golden brown in color and the flesh is white and flaky. Do not overcrowd the pan. When the fish is done, transfer the pieces to a paper towel-lined plate to drain. Serve hot.

Crab Mornay

Serves 8
Cooking Time: 30 minutes

6 tablespoons (¾ stick) unsalted butter
1 medium onion, diced
¾ pound button mushrooms, stemmed and sliced ⅛-inch thick
6 tablespoons all-purpose flour
½ cup chicken broth
½ cup heavy cream
6 ounces grated Gruyere cheese
4 ounces grated Parmesan cheese
1 tablespoon dry sherry
Salt, to taste
Cayenne pepper, to taste
2 pounds fresh lump crab meat, picked clean

Preheat the oven to 350 degrees F.

In a skillet or sauté pan, melt the butter over medium heat and sauté the onions and mushrooms for 3 to 4 minutes, or until soft. Stir in the flour until smooth, then add the chicken broth and stir until thickened and smooth. Add the cream and both cheeses, and stir until the cheeses melt and the sauce becomes thick and smooth. Remove from the heat and add the dry sherry. Season with salt and cayenne pepper to taste. Fold in the crab meat and spoon the mixture into a 9 x 13-inch greased casserole dish. Bake for 20 minutes or until the casserole is bubbly.

Momma's Meatloaf

Serves 4 to 6
Cooking Time: 75 minutes

2 pounds lean ground beef
1 cup bread crumbs
1 medium yellow onion, diced
1 egg, beaten
1½ teaspoons salt
¼ teaspoon pepper
1 (16-ounce) can tomato sauce

Sauce
1 (16-ounce can) tomato sauce
2 tablespoons vinegar
3 tablespoons light brown sugar
2 tablespoons Worcestershire sauce
2 teaspoons yellow mustard

Preheat the oven to 350 degrees F.

Mix the beef, bread crumbs, onion, egg, salt, pepper, and tomato sauce and stir until well combined. Press the mixture into a greased loaf pan, or form it into a loaf and bake it on a greased sheet pan.

To make the sauce, mix the tomato sauce, vinegar, brown sugar, Worcestershire sauce, yellow mustard, and ½ cup water in a separate bowl and pour over the beef mixture. Bake, uncovered, for 75 to 85 minutes.

My mother wasn't a very good cook, but this is one dish she could always be proud of. I like to bake this on a big cookie sheet instead of a loaf pan so that it's crusty all over. Feel free to use more sauce on it after it's finished cooking, if you want more flavor.

M Street Meatballs

This is a fantastic, lighter version of a traditional meatball recipe. We braise them in stock and allow them to cool without an actual sauce, and you can use the braising liquid as a base for a simple pan sauce. They are perfect when they are warm and served with potatoes, or simply sliced and used for sandwiches.

Serves 6
Cooking Time: 35 minutes

1½ pounds ground turkey breast
1 large egg
2 cups fresh bread crumbs
1½ tablespoons Dijon mustard
1 teaspoon cayenne pepper
1 teaspoon kosher salt
1 teaspoon black pepper
6 cups chicken stock (or enough
    to fill the pot with ½ inch of liquid)

In a large bowl, stir together the turkey, egg, bread crumbs, mustard, cayenne, salt, pepper, and ½ cup warm water. Shape the meat mixture into meatballs approximately 2 ½ inches in diameter and set aside.

In a large pot, heat the chicken stock to boiling and then reduce the heat to medium. Using tongs, carefully arrange the meatballs in the hot liquid and cook the meatballs for 20 minutes. Turn the meatballs and continue cooking for 15 minutes, or until they are cooked through.

Transfer the meatballs to a large plate and allow them to rest at least 15 minutes before slicing or serving. If desired, take the liquid from the pan and serve it as a sauce. I personally prefer to serve these with a marinara or barbecue sauce.

Beef and Wine

Serves 6 to 7
Cooking Time: 35 minutes

½ cup chopped onions
½ cup chopped celery
½ cup chopped bell pepper
2 tablespoons olive oil
3 garlic cloves
½ cup red wine
1½ cups beef stock
1 tablespoon Worcestershire sauce
1 bay leaf
1 teaspoon angostura bitters
8 ounces white mushrooms, sliced
1 teaspoon salt
1 teaspoon black pepper
1½ pounds cubed leftover roast beef

Sauté the onion, celery, and bell pepper in olive oil over medium heat for 2 to 3 minutes, or until soft, then add the garlic cloves and continue to cook for 2 more minutes. Add the red wine and cook for 2 to 3 minutes over high heat to cook off the alcohol. Stir in the stock, Worcestershire sauce, bay leaf, bitters, mushrooms, salt, and pepper and allow to simmer for another 3 minutes.

Add the leftover roast beef and continue to simmer over medium heat for 20 minutes.

I like to serve this over rice with a nice crisp green salad. Big Momma likes it served with a side of mash potatoes.

When I was a kid we were in what we now call economically challenged circumstances. In other words, we were poor and had to eat the leftovers before our momma could afford to cook something new. Hence, I grew to hate leftovers. Since then I have changed my tune. Nowadays, I like to recycle leftovers into something totally different. That's what this recipe is all about. Whenever I have leftover prime rib, pot roast, or even tenderloin, I freeze it and bring it out for this dish a month later.

When people come over to my house, they generally expect me to cook out. I live in a highrise in Dallas and don't have the space to have a smoker, so I have developed some recipes that can be cooked in the oven just as well as in the smoker, without having access to the outside barbecue pit.

Oklahoma Hot Steaks

I made this recipe on the Regis and Kelly show once (see p. 104). It's a great recipe to make at home, too.

Serves 6 to 7

6 (12-ounce) rib eye steaks
1 jar sliced jalapeños, plus the juice
3 fresh jalapeño peppers, stemmed and sliced
2 ounces olive oil

Place the steaks in a 1-gallon plastic bag. Add the juice from the jar of jalapeños into the bag, along with half the sliced jalapeño peppers.

Chop the raw jalapeños and add them, along with the olive oil, to the bag. Seal the gallon bag and turn several times to make sure the ingredients are mixed. Refrigerate overnight. On the day of your party, remove the steaks from the bag and allow them to sit out and come to room temperature, at least one hour.

Cook the steaks for 3 to 4 minutes on each side over a hot grill for a medium steak. If you're cooking the steaks inside, place them on a broiler pan and broil them in the oven on high for 3 minutes. Then turn them over and cook for 3 more minutes on the other side. The steaks at this point will be medium to medium well. Reduce the cooking time if you wish the steaks to be more rare.

Note: If you want the recipe to be less spicy, omit the raw jalapeños. These were included for Big Momma, since she is from New Mexico and is a fan of hot food. Also, remember to use rubber gloves when handling raw chicken and/or jalapeño peppers. Don't forget to season the steaks well with sea salt and, of course, pepper before serving.

"Live with Regis & Kelly" featuring Dickey's Barbecue

In the summer of 2004 the folks from "Live With Regis & Kelly" called to ask if we'd like to come to New York to cook for a barbecue segment that the show was planning. Roland Jr. and I flew to New York to prepare "Oklahoma Hot Steaks," a dish that is outstanding because the meat is marinated overnight or for a few hours in jalapeño juice. The crew set up a grill outside, which was interesting with all the happenings on the busy streets of the Big Apple. We had a great time and Regis and Kelly were really kind to us.

The show's producer, Michael Gelman, is a real gentleman. I'm sure he sees rubes like me from the country all the time, but instead of acting like a sophisticated New Yorker, he comes across as a regular guy. We had loads of fun until my son and I decided to move a few bowls of fruit that were decorating the serving table near where we were cooking. As soon as Roland and I picked up the bowls, the assistant director hollered at us to put them down. Unbeknownst to us, we were violating the union rule that says only union members can pick up props on set. I guess there's some truth in the saying, "you learn something new every day," because that sure was news to me.

Food Show Chicken

Serves 4

2 tablespoons flour
1 teaspoon Cajun seasoning
1 whole chicken, cut in pieces
2 tablespoons olive oil
1 cup chopped green onions
½ cup white wine
2 cups chicken stock
1 cup frozen peas
1 (8-ounce) package white mushrooms, sliced
5 to 6 medium new potatoes
1½ teaspoons salt
12 turns black pepper from peppermill
1 tablespoon garlic paste
1 bay leaf
1 teaspoon dry sweet basil
1 teaspoon Louisiana hot sauce

Mix the flour and Cajun seasoning, then dredge the chicken pieces in the flour and shake to remove any excess. Heat the olive oil in a skillet over medium-high heat, and brown the chicken on all sides, turning at least once. When the chicken is beginning to brown but not completely done, transfer it to paper towels to drain.

Sauté the chopped green onions in the skillet for 2 minutes, add the white wine, and cook for 2 to 3 more minutes. Add the chicken stock along with the peas, mushrooms, and potatoes. Cook for 2 to 3 minutes more, then stir in the bay leaf, sweet basil, and Louisiana hot sauce, and return the chicken to the skillet. Cover and cook for 45 minutes over medium heat, or until the chicken is cooked thoroughly and the potatoes are tender.

When the chicken is completely done and tender, turn off the stove and leave the covered skillet to rest on the stovetop for 10 minutes before serving.

Note: This recipe can be held in a warm oven for an hour before serving, if you make it ahead of time.

During the annual restaurant food show held in Chicago every May, I always eat at the same restaurant—an Italian restaurant called Carmines. They have a chicken dish very similar to a dish on our menu. If you're in Chicago you should try this dish—or just cook it yourself at home. It is a great recipe for the family—it's very inexpensive because chicken on the bone is much cheaper than buying the boneless breasts.

Garlic Steaks

Serves 6

6 (12-ounce) rib eye steaks or New York strips
1 tube garlic paste
4 tablespoons dry steak rub, divided (recipe, p. 49)

Rub the steaks with the garlic paste and 2 tablespoons of the steak rub and refrigerate for 2 to 3 hours, or overnight. An hour prior to cooking, remove the steaks from the refrigerator and season again with the remaining 2 tablespoons of dry steak rub.

Broil the steaks in an oven, or on an outside grill, for 3 to 4 minutes, then turn and repeat on the other side for a medium-rare doneness. Dust the steaks lightly with salt before serving.

How to Host a Cook-Out

I was born and bred in Dallas but own a second home in Santa Fe because Big Momma, my wife (whose real name is Maurine), is from New Mexico. Whenever folks come over to our Santa Fe house, they expect to see me cooking out because, obviously, that's the nature of my business. After all, as somebody always says, "We don't go to the barbecue king's house for fried chicken or tofu." As usual, I have a few tips for hosting a cook-out that will please your guests as well as you so you won't be totally knocked out by all the work.

★ If possible, avoid cooking individual steaks. If you do, people will stand over you and pester you about how they want their meat cooked. Take it from me—this puts a big burden on you as a host. Cook something at a barbecue that you've smoked all day—something like a brisket, ribs, or chicken halves. Chicken halves are great because everyone eats them the same way (well done) and they're inexpensive.

★ If you must have steaks, spend the money and select whole tenderloin. Cook it on medium rare and you still have part of it medium well on each end. Slice it right before serving, but be warned—a whole tenderloin will cost major doe-ray-me.

★ Have the smoked meat totally cooked before guests arrive, but leave it on the outside grill on a very low temperature just enough to stay warm. This serves a dual purpose: it lets your friends know how much work you've done plus they get to see and smell the delicious items on the grill. This always drives up their appetites.

★ Purchase prepared garlic bread and dessert. People will never appreciate the work that goes into actually making these two items so do it the easy way. Unwrap the garlic bread, put it in tin foil with a little extra melted butter or olive oil or parmesan cheese on top and your guests will think you've made it from scratch. The same goes for cake or pies. Take them out of the store-bought boxes and serve them on one of your plates. Just be sure to get rid of all the "evidence" before the guests arrive.

★ The one thing you're going to prepare after the guests walk in will be a salad of some sort. People love to stand around and watch you create this, so gather around your kitchen counter or island and pour everyone a glass of wine while you prepare the salad. It's a great time for sharing. Let them refill their own wine glasses.

★ Once the salad is ready, put everything on the counter and have your guests serve themselves buffet-style.

★ Offer white or red wine, and bottled water. If somebody wants a cocktail, you can mix it or better yet let them make it themselves. If you have bottles of wine sitting around, people will tend bar themselves. You don't want to mix a cocktail every time someone finishes a drink.

★ Eight is the ideal number for a dinner party. This includes you and your significant other and six other guests. More than eight makes the job big and the clean-up even bigger. I don't like to have just one couple over because there is too little to talk about. Two couples are great, three is better but four is definitely a crowd.

Porcupines

Serves 4
Cooking Time: 45 minutes to 1 hour

1 pound lean ground sirloin
1 egg, lightly beaten
2 tablespoons bread crumbs
1 teaspoon salt
1 teaspoon black pepper
½ cup long grain white rice, uncooked
2 tablespoons ketchup
1 (10-ounce) can red enchilada sauce

Preheat the oven to 350 degrees F.

Combine the sirloin, egg, bread crumbs, salt, pepper, rice, and ketchup and mix well. Shape the meat mixture into 6 round porcupine balls. Place them in a Pyrex baking dish and cover with the red enchilada sauce. Be sure to spoon at least 2 tablespoons of enchilada sauce over each porcupine. Cover the baking dish with tin foil and bake for 45 minutes to 1 hour.

In New Mexico, these are always served over Spanish rice or refried beans.

This is a dish Big Momma grew up eating in New Mexico. It's different from any other kind of meatloaf I've ever tasted. This can be served with a mild or hot sauce.

Chicken in Foil

Serves 6

1½ pounds chicken breast
1 tablespoon Cajun seasoning
3 cups new potatoes, sliced
2 cups carrot, sliced
1 large onion, sliced
5 to 6 cloves garlic, crushed
1 (10-ounce) packaged frozen English peas

Cut up the chicken into 6 individual portions and rub with the Cajun seasoning. Cut 6 pieces of tin foil, about 12 inches long each, and place ½ cup sliced potato, ⅓ cup sliced carrot, a slice of raw onion, one garlic pod, and 2 to 3 tablespoons of English peas in each packet, along with a piece of raw chicken breast. Seal up the packets well and place in refrigerator. Forget about them until the next night.

The next night when you rush home from work, preheat the oven to 350 degrees F. Place the packets in the oven and cook for 1 hour. When these are finished cooking the garlic and Cajun seasoning will give you a great smell in the kitchen.

Be sure to check one of the packs before you serve to make sure the chicken and vegetables are done. I like to let each person open one of these up individually on his own plate. That way he gets the great smell of the chicken and vegetables, and kids love it because it is something unusual to do. Let them eat it right out of the tin foil with a piece of French breach to soak up the great juices. They will love this dish and it's a great shortcut to having a homemade dinner.

This is a great recipe you can make without having to spend much time in the kitchen. If you make it the night before, you can cook it when you get home from work. It's based on an old recipe from my brief days as a boy scout. Unfortunately, I was kicked out of the scouts because of running a card game out of my tent—but that's another story.

Chicken Pot Pie

Yields 1 (9-inch) pie
Cooking Time: 45 minutes

2 prepared pie crusts
1½ tablespoons butter
1 tablespoon chopped onion
2 tablespoons flour
1½ cups milk
1 (10-ounce) package frozen peas and carrots
1½ cups chicken, cooked and diced
¼ teaspoon thyme
Salt and pepper, to taste
1 egg, beaten

Line a pie pan with one pie crust, allowing the edges to spill over the edge of the dish, and set aside.

Melt the butter in a saucepan. Add the onion and sauté until translucent. Stir in the flour and add the milk. Reduce the heat and continue cooking until the mixture has thickened.

Add the peas, carrots, chicken, thyme, salt, and pepper and remove from the heat. Place the filling into the pie crust and brush the edges of the pie crust with the egg. Cover the dish with the second pie crust. Using a knife, cut around the edge to remove the extra crust and crimp the edge with a fork all around to seal the top and bottom together.

Cut 3 small vents in the center of the crust to allow steam to escape while cooking. Brush the top of the pie with more of the egg and cook in a 350-degree F oven for 45 minutes, or until the crust is golden brown.

Smothered Steak Edna

We named this recipe after Edna, a zany character featured on our YouTube channel and our website. If you have never looked at our website or Dickey's YouTube channel, be sure to do so—I think you'll get a laugh. Edna's from a small town in Texas called Italy, and she loves this kind of heavy food, bless her heart.

Serves 4

5 tablespoons flour
1 teaspoon salt
1 teaspoon pepper
4 (8-ounce) steaks, cubed
4 tablespoons olive oil
1 cup chopped onion
3 cloves garlic, crushed
3 tablespoons dry sherry, or plain dry white wine
2 cups beef stock
1 package brown gravy mix (any brand will do—I generally use McCormick or Knorr)
8 ounces mushrooms, sliced

Season the flour with salt and pepper and dredge the steaks in it. Heat the olive oil in a skillet over medium heat and brown the steaks for about 3 to 4 minutes per side. Transfer the steaks to a plate and allow them to rest.

Add the onion and garlic to the skillet and cook for 2 minutes. Add the dry sherry and cook for a few minutes to cook off the alcohol. Add the stock and the gravy mix according to the package directions.

Return the steak to the skillet, add the sliced mushrooms, and turn the heat down to low. Cook for 30 minutes, or until the smothered steaks are tender. If the gravy gets too thick, thin it out with a little more stock or water.

When the steaks are tender, serve with mashed potatoes or cooked white rice and a salad. While this recipe is cooking on the stove, it's a great time to have a glass of wine with your husband or wife.

Good Friends

I've known former restaurateur Joanna Windham for years and asked her a while back if she'd like to help me with a unique advertising gimmick for Dickey's. We created a zany character called Edna that Joanna plays in Dickey's commercials on YouTube. If you've never seen our website (www.dickeys.com) which has a link to YouTube, be sure to do so because watching Edna will make you laugh. Joanna is from a small town called Italy, Texas, and she loves heavy cooking. Smothered steak is one of her favorites (recipe, p. 114).

Located across the street from our corporate offices in Dallas, Adelmo's restaurant is owned by good friends, Adelmo Bancheti, his wife Leiza, and their two children, Lauren and Andrew. It has become our unofficial family living room. This restaurant is never open unless one of the Banchetis is there overseeing operations.

Adelmo's is truly a family-owned restaurant in the best sense of the word. In fact, the Dickey's movers and shakers meet there weekly to go over operating results from the prior week. When my son Cullen began searching for larger office space for us, he asked my opinion. I told him, "You can locate it anywhere you want to as long as it is within walking distance of Adelmo's."

I also love meeting folks at our grand openings all over the country. This has become my favorite part of the job today.

Sarah's Chicken Casserole

Serves 4 to 6

1 whole medium chicken
4 ounces (1 stick) unsalted butter
2½ cups herb-seasoned bread stuffing
1 (12-ounce) can cream of celery soup
1 (12-ounce) can cream of chicken soup
8 ounces sour cream

Sarah's an old friend of Big Momma's. I think she's a politician, too, so you know she must love to eat.

In a stockpot, boil the whole chicken for 45 minutes, or until tender. Remove the skin and bones and shred the meat into small pieces. Reserve the broth (see note).

Melt the butter in a saucepan and mix thoroughly with 2 cups of the stuffing mix. Pour the stuffing mixture into the bottom of a 9 x 13-inch baking pan. Cover the mixture entirely with the shredded chicken.

In a separate bowl, mix together the cream of celery soup, cream of chicken soup, and the sour cream. Pour over the chicken.

Use the remaining stuffing mixture to cover the cream layer with a top layer of stuffing mix. Bake uncovered for 20 to 25 minutes, or until the stuffing top begins to brown.

Note: For a softer top layer, pour 1 cup of warm chicken broth over the stuffing mix before baking.

Brisket Tacos

Serves 4

1 small yellow onion, julienned
1 jalapeño, seeded if desired
1 pound cooked brisket, shredded
6 corn or flour tortillas
1 cup shredded lettuce, for garnish
½ cup shredded cheddar cheese, for garnish
1 Roma tomato, seeded and julienned

Sauté the onion and jalapeño in a skillet for 3 to 5 minutes, or until soft. Add the brisket to the skillet and heat through. While the meat is warming, heat 6 corn or flour tortillas in a separate skillet or a microwave. Distribute the meat mixture evenly among the tortillas, and garnish with lettuce, cheddar cheese, and tomato.

Adelmo's Garlic Chicken

Serves 4 to 6

1/2 cup extra virgin olive oil
Juice of 2 lemons
1 tablespoon thyme
1 tablespoon allspice
4 chicken breasts, skin on, cut "airplane" style
Kosher salt and black pepper, to taste

In a large bowl, combine the olive oil, lemon juice, thyme, and allspice to make a marinade. Add the chicken breasts to the marinade and refrigerate overnight.

When you are ready to prepare the garlic chicken, salt and pepper both sides of the marinated meat and place on a sheet pan or casserole dish. Bake in a preheated 350-degree oven for 30 minutes. Heat the remaining marinade in a saucepan over medium heat, salt and pepper to taste, and use as a sauce for the baked chicken.

DICKEY'S BARBECUE
Since ★ 1941
HOWDY
neighbor

GREAT-TASTIN'
SIDE DISHES
AND VEGGIES

Barbecue Beans

Serves 6 to 8

1 slice Applewood bacon
3 tablespoons maple syrup
5 tablespoons light brown sugar
2 teaspoons yellow mustard
½ teaspoon smoked paprika
1 teaspoon molasses
1½ teaspoons liquid smoke (available
   in your grocer's sauce aisle)
2 teaspoons apple cider vinegar
¼ cup beef broth
1 (28-ounce) can pork n' beans
Kosher salt, to taste
Cracked black pepper, to taste

Cut the slice of bacon in half and sauté it in a medium pot over low heat. Render the bacon for 7 to 8 minutes, stirring every 2 minutes.

While the bacon is rendering, mix together the syrup, brown sugar, mustard, paprika, molasses, liquid smoke, vinegar, and beef broth in a large bowl. Set aside.

Once the bacon is rendered, add the mixed ingredients to the pot, and stir for 10 seconds to deglaze the pan. Add the pork n' beans and stir. Allow the beans to simmer on medium-low heat for 10 minutes. Season to taste and serve.

Green Beans with Bacon

Serves 4 to 6

2 slices smoked Applewood bacon, ½-inch dice
¼ cup (½ stick) unsalted butter
3 cloves fresh garlic, minced
⅓ cup yellow onions, ½-inch dice
⅓ cup Dickey's Smoked Ham, ¼-inch dice
1 (28-ounce) package frozen Italian cut green
    beans, or 15 ounces fresh green beans (see note)
Kosher salt, to taste
Cracked black pepper, to taste

Heat the diced bacon in a medium stockpot on low heat for 8 to 10 minutes to render the fat, stirring every 2 minutes. Once the bacon is fully rendered, turn the heat up to medium-high and add the butter. When the butter fully melts, add the garlic and onions and cook for 3 to 4 minutes, or until a caramel color is achieved.

Add the smoked ham and continue to cook, stirring, for 2 minutes. Add the green beans to the pot, and stir well to combine. Bring the beans to a boil, and simmer for 10 minutes. Season to taste, remove from the heat, and serve hot.

Note: If you use fresh green beans, use about 3 ounces per person. Snap off the ends, and remove the "string." Bring 2 quarts of water to a boil in a large stockpot, and add 2 teaspoons of kosher salt. Add ½ cup chicken stock to the pot before boiling. Blanch the beans in the boiling water for 45 seconds to 1 minute, then drain and submerge the beans in an icewater bath.

Jalapeño Beans

Serves 4 to 6

1 tablespoon canola oil
¼ cup yellow onion, finely minced
2 tablespoons white vinegar
3 tablespoons pickled jalapeños, diced
½ teaspoon Tabasco sauce
1 teaspoon ground cumin
½ teaspoon chili powder
½ teaspoon garlic powder
¼ cup Shiner Bock beer
½ teaspoon smoked paprika
¼ teaspoon cayenne pepper
1 (28-ounce) can chili beans
Kosher salt, to taste
Cracked black pepper, to taste

Heat the canola oil and minced onions in a medium stockpot over low heat. Cook the onions for 1 to 2 minutes, stirring continuously.

In a separate bowl, mix all the ingredients except the chili beans. Add the mixture to the pot and cook for 30 seconds, then add in the chili beans and stir well. Continue to simmer on medium-low heat for 10 minutes. Season to taste and serve.

Jalapeño Cream Corn

Serves 4 to 6
Cooking Time: 20 minutes

4 ears Olathe sweet corn, unshucked
1 tablespoon unsalted butter
3 to 4 cloves fresh garlic, minced
1 fresh jalapeño, seeded, ⅛-inch dice
1 cup heavy cream
4 ounces cream cheese
½ teaspoon ground cumin
Kosher salt, to taste
Cracked black pepper, to taste

Garnish
1 Roma tomato, seeded, ¼-inch dice
1 bunch fresh cilantro, stemmed and minced,
    or green onions

Soak the unshucked ears of corn in water for 10 minutes. Once the corn is done soaking, heat an outdoor grill to high, and roast the corn on the grill for 13 to 15 minutes, or until the kernels of corn start to turn red and tan. Remove the corn from the heat, and transfer to a cutting board. Remove the husks, and the "strings" from the ears, and discard.

Cut the corn kernels from the cob, and place into a separate bowl.

Melt the butter in a medium saucepan over medium-high heat. Add the garlic and jalapeño and cook, stirring, until the garlic turns light brown, about 1 minute. Add the corn kernels, and cook for 2 more minutes, stirring continuously. Add the heavy cream, cream cheese, and cumin, and continue to stir until the cream cheese has melted. Lower the heat, and simmer for 2 more minutes. Garnish with fresh cilantro and tomatoes and serve.

No doubt about it, Bill Richardson is a great guy

A great politician who Maurine and I count as our friend is Bill Richardson, who has had an illustrious career as Ambassador to the United Nations, two-time governor of New Mexico, and former Congressman, among other important jobs. He is a totally brilliant man and would have made a great president. He's also a Democrat.

We came to know Bill and his wife Barbara in Santa Fe, New Mexico, where we have another house. In fact, Maurine and I hosted a fund-raiser for Bill when he ran for governor in 2002—and the media jumped all over us. When Maurine declared she was running for office in 2004, newspaper stories claimed that "in Dallas she is a Republican but in New Mexico she's a Democrat." The truth is that my wife and I believe more in the person than the party. Bill Richardson would be an asset to this country as either a Democrat or a Republican.

He and I agree on a lot of important things, not the least of which is this Jalapeño Cream Corn Soup, which we both love.

Chardonnay Carrots

This is a great way to eat carrots. Don't forget you can buy baby carrots already peeled and ready to go if you don't like to use whole carrots.

Serves 4 to 6
Cooking Time: 12 to 15 minutes

¼ cup (½ stick) unsalted butter, melted
1 cup white wine
1 ounce white wine vinegar
1 teaspoon fresh thyme, chopped
Kosher salt, to taste
Cracked black pepper, to taste
1 pound baby carrots, stem on, washed
Fresh tarragon leaves, chopped, for garnish

In a large mixing bowl, combine the butter, wine, white wine vinegar, thyme, salt, and black pepper. Add the carrots and allow them to marinate out at room temperature for 1 hour.

Preheat the oven to 400 degrees F.

Use a piece of foil to make a "bowl" and pour the carrots and juice into it. Seal the foil bowl so that it does not leak, place it in glass pie plate or on an aluminum sheet pan, and bake for 12 to 15 minutes, or until just tender.

Garnish with fresh tarragon leaves and serve.

Momma's Mac

Serves 4 to 6

1½ cups elbow pasta
2 tablespoons (¼ stick) butter
3 slices bacon, ¼-inch dice
2 eggs
4 ounces evaporated milk
½ cup chicken stock
2 teaspoons Knorr dry chicken base
1 teaspoon kosher salt
1 teaspoon black pepper
2 ounces cream cheese
2 ounces Velveeta
8 ounces sharp cheddar cheese, shredded
⅓ cup Goldfish crackers
⅓ cup Ritz crackers

Cook the pasta per the instructions on the box. The cook time is usually 8 to 10 minutes. Drain the pasta, and keep pasta in a colander.

As the pasta is boiling, render the bacon pieces. Place the raw bacon into a medium stockpot on low heat and cook, stirring every 2 minutes. The bacon will turn a burgundy color, and it will render out the clear bacon fat. When the bacon is fully rendered, remove the bacon from the heat and drain off the bacon fat. Return the bacon pieces to the pot.

To prepare the cheese sauce, mix the eggs, evaporated milk, chicken stock, chicken base, salt, and pepper in a separate bowl. Whisk well until the ingredients are fully incorporated. Add this mixture to the bacon and whisk over medium heat for 2 minutes. Add the cream cheese, Velveeta, and cheddar cheese to the bacon mixture. Continue to whisk until all the cheese has melted, and the cheese sauce is smooth.

Add the pasta into the cheese sauce, and toss well to coat. Cook for 1 minute more, and add the garnish.

To make the garnish, place the Goldfish and Ritz crackers in a food processor, and pulse to lightly chop. Sprinkle this mixture over the top of Momma's Mac and enjoy!

Broccoli Casserole (the right way!)

Serves 4 to 6
Cooking Time: 30 minutes

4 heads fresh broccoli
1½ tablespoons cornstarch
½ cup milk
3 eggs, beaten
1½ cups ricotta cheese
⅓ cup cheddar cheese, grated
1 medium yellow onion, ⅛-inch dice
Salt, to taste
Cracked black pepper, to taste

Preheat the oven to 350 degrees F.

Rinse the broccoli, and remove and discard the leaves. Boil the heads and stalks of the broccoli in enough water to cover for 10 minutes. Drain the broccoli and chop it coarsely, including the stalks.

In a small bowl, dissolve the cornstarch in the milk. In a separate bowl, beat the eggs. Add the eggs, ricotta, cheddar cheese, and the cornstarch-milk mixture and mix thoroughly. Add the chopped onion, salt, and pepper. Stir in the drained, chopped broccoli, and blend the ingredients well.

Place the broccoli mixture into an ovenproof baking dish and bake for 30 minutes, or until bubbly. Serve hot.

Big Momma will eat broccoli anyway she wants to. If you don't like broccoli—I don't like it myself—you will like it this way. It's about the only way I will eat it. Even kids will eat this recipe.

The Best Mashed Potatoes

Serves 4 to 6

5 pounds russet potatoes
4 ounces (1 stick) unsalted butter
1½ cups sour cream
2 pints whole milk
Kosher salt, to taste
Black pepper, finely ground, to taste

Garnish
1 bunch green onions, green parts only, ¼-inch slices
½ cup shredded cheddar cheese
4 strips bacon, crisply cooked and crumbled

Preheat the oven to 350 degrees F.

Wash the potatoes under cool running water, and pat dry. Place the potatoes on a sheet tray, and cook for 70 to 90 minutes.

Remove the potatoes from the oven, carefully place each in a kitchen towel, and rub off the skin while the potatoes are still warm. Discard the skins. Chop the potatoes into 1-inch pieces and place them into a large bowl. Using an electric hand mixer or a potato masher, mash the potatoes with the butter, sour cream, and milk until smooth. Season to taste with salt and pepper, and garnish with green onions, cheddar cheese, and crumbled bacon.

Marshall Mills' Turkey Dressing

Serves 8 to 10

½ cup (1 stick) butter
1½ cups chopped celery
1½ cups chopped onions
8 cups crumbled cornmeal cornbread (made from scratch or a mix)
2 eggs, slightly beaten
4 heaping tablespoons chopped sage (some folks like more)
4 cups chicken broth
1 teaspoon salt
1 teaspoon black pepper

Grease a 9 x 13-inch baking pan and preheat the oven to 350 degrees F.

Melt the butter in a skillet over medium-low heat and sauté the onion and celery for 5 to 10 minutes, or until tender. Prepare the cornbread according to the package directions. Crumble the cornbread into a large bowl. In a separate bowl, whip the eggs and sage into the chicken broth and pour over the cornbread. Add the onions and celery and season to taste. Bake for 45 minutes, uncovered. (If you prefer a less moist cornbread dressing, crush in some saltine crackers to absorb the juices.)

This is Marshall Mills' Turkey Dressing Recipe (as related to him by his grandmother, Ollie Rich Dickey). This recipe comes originally from my mother, and she gave it to my nephew, Marshall Mills. Marshall is a big-time real estate executive, but he is also a dressing lover and a great cook in his own right. We serve this recipe every Christmas with our turkey.

Variations

Through the years as this recipe has passed into family hands, many different things have been added:

1 cup chopped or shredded Dickey's barbecue ham
1 cup golden raisins
4 hardboiled eggs, chopped
1 pound Dickey's Barbecue sausage, chopped (pretty spicy!)
1 cup cooked, chopped mushrooms (someone married a Yankee, what can I say?)

DICKEY'S BARBECUE

Since ★ 1941

HOWDY

neighbor

EYE-OPENIN'
BREAKFAST
AND BREADS

Grits Casserole

This dish is great served with scrambled eggs and biscuits or toast.

Serves 6

2 cups old-fashioned grits, uncooked (not instant)
1 pound cooked breakfast sausage
1 Kraft garlic cheese log (available in your grocer's cheese section), or 6 ounces Velveeta
2 ounces jalapeño peppers, sliced
Black pepper, to taste
2 eggs, beaten
1 cup shredded cheddar cheese

Preheat the oven to 350 degrees F.

Follow the package directions to cook the grits. (Remember to always cook the grits covered.) When the grits are done, pour them into a large mixing bowl. Add the cooked breakfast sausage (I prefer Jimmy Dean's hot, but use your favorite), the garlic cheese log or Velveeta, the jalapeño peppers, black pepper to taste, and the eggs. Blend all the ingredients into the cooked grits and pour into a large Pyrex baking dish. Cover with shredded cheddar cheese and bake, uncovered, in the oven for 30 minutes.

Leftover Sausage Omelet

When you have some leftover sausage from Dickey's or anywhere else, it's great to use it the next day in an omelet.

Serves 1

1 tablespoon olive oil, or canola oil, or
   a mixture of canola oil and butter
2 tablespoons bell peppers, chopped, per omelet
Chopped leftover sausage
2 to 3 large eggs
1 tablespoon half-and-half
Salt and pepper, to taste

Put enough oil in a hot skillet to coat and sauté the peppers for 2 to 3 minutes, or until they become soft. Add the sausage to the skillet and continue to cook for 2 to 3 minutes more.

In a separate bowl, beat the eggs and 1 tablespoon of half-and-half. Once the sausage and peppers are tender, add the egg mixture to the skillet with salt and pepper to taste and continue to cook to your desired doneness, folding the edges over gently when the omelet has cooked.

Note: If you don't want to take the time to make an omelet, you can follow this recipe but just scramble the eggs with the sausage and peppers. It tastes the same, but it's not as pretty.

Pigs in a Blanket

Serves 4

1 can Pillsbury pop-up biscuit dough
1 package link sausage
1 small bottle Louisiana hot sauce

Preheat the oven to 350 degrees F.

Cook the sausage according to the package and set aside.

Roll out each piece of biscuit dough to a flat round. Place 1 sausage link in each dough round and generously coat with the hot sauce. Roll the link in the dough and place each "pig in a blanket" on a cookie sheet. Bake in the oven according to the biscuit package instructions, until the dough expands and is nicely browned.

Some people like to brush the dough with butter to make it brown even more.

This is a great breakfast dish that can also be served, believe it or not, at a cocktail party. Especially at a cocktail party where you need a lot of carbs going into people's stomachs to slow down their joy (if you know what I mean).

Ham and Red-Eye Gravy

This makes a spicy, hot, different sort of ham and red-eye gravy that you will love!

Serves 2
Cooking Time: 5 minutes

1 tablespoon olive or canola oil
1 pound ham steak, cut in 5 to 6 pieces
1 teaspoon paprika
½ teaspoon cayenne pepper
½ teaspoon black pepper
4 tablespoons brewed coffee

Heat the olive oil in a skillet over medium heat and cook the ham for 3 to 4 minutes, turning, until the pieces are hot. Add the paprika, cayenne, black pepper, and ¼ cup water to the skillet and continue to cook for 3 to 4 minutes, or until the liquid has reduced. Add the hot coffee and cook for 2 to 3 minutes more and serve.

Maple-Sage Cornbread

Serves 6 to 8
Cooking Time: 12 to 15 minutes

1 (6-ounce) package yellow cornbread mix
¼ cup maple syrup
1 teaspoon fresh sage, finely chopped

Prepare the cornbread according to the package instructions, adding the maple syrup and sage to the batter. Bake in a 350-degree F oven for 12 to 15 minutes, or until the top begins to brown.

Jalapeño-Cheese Cornbread

Serves 6 to 8
Cooking Time: 12 to 15 minutes

1 (6-ounce) package yellow cornbread mix
½ cup shredded cheddar cheese
2 tablespoons pickled jalapeño, finely chopped and patted dry

Prepare the cornbread according to the package instructions, adding the cheese and jalapeño to the batter. Bake in a 350-degree F oven for 12 to 15 minutes, or until the top begins to brown.

Sausage Egg Casserole

Serves 4

3 cups seasoned croutons
1 pound ground sausage
2 cups shredded cheddar cheese
1 can cream of mushroom soup
2 cups milk
8 eggs
¾ teaspoon dry mustard
¼ pound mushrooms, ⅛-inch slice
¼ cup (½ stick) unsalted butter

My mother loves this recipe and she loved anything that has cream of mushroom soup in it.

The night before you plan to serve, place the croutons in the bottom of a 9 x 13-inch baking dish. In a skillet, brown the sausage. Drain the cooked sausage and crumble it over the croutons. In a separate bowl whisk together the cheese, soup, milk, eggs, and dry mustard. Pour the egg mixture over the sausage.

In a large skillet, sauté the mushrooms in butter until they are fully cooked. Add the mushrooms to the casserole, stir, and refrigerate, covered, overnight. Just before you are ready to serve, preheat an oven to 300 degrees F. Bake the casserole for 1 hour and serve hot.

Garlic Texas Toast on the Grill

Serves 4 to 6

1 loaf Texas Toast
2 tablespoons olive oil
2 cloves chopped garlic, or garlic powder
Parmesan cheese, optional

Get rid of the Texas Toast wrapper, and place the loaf of bread on enough tin foil to completely cover it. Using your hand or a brush, lightly glaze the loaf of bread on all sides with olive oil. Rub the chopped garlic on the loaf, or sprinkle the loaf with garlic powder. If you like Parmesan cheese, this is another good addition to sprinkle on top. Wrap the loaf up tightly and cook outside on the grill until the bread is nice and crunchy.

If you have already read other parts of this cookbook, you'll notice I suggest you never make homemade bread for a dinner party. What you want to do instead is buy a loaf of prepared Texas Toast (I like the New York brand, but others are equally good). People will like this bread whether it's homemade or not. It's especially delish with steaks!

Celebrities, Politics, and Texas Toast

In Dallas, my wife and I have long been known as Republicans. I am a former Republican county chairman for one of our suburban counties and, for more than seven years my wife Maurine has been a Dallas County Commissioner representing roughly 620,000 residents. The entire Dickey family and I are extremely proud of her and support her motto of always putting taxpayers first. She is the epitome of the elected official who tries to do what's best for the small businessman and the little guy.

Another politician I've known for years is Ross Perot who tossed his hat into the Presidential ring in 1992. I met Mr. Perot way before then because he has been a great customer of Dickey's for many years. I happen to know that Mr. Perot gives his time and money to plenty of charitable causes without expecting anything—including recognition—in return.

For example, after the 1991 Gulf War, 10,000 returning troops came into Dallas on buses from various military posts for a celebratory march through downtown. City officials nearly had egg on their collective faces when they realized that no lunches were to be provided to the hungry soldiers. Ross Perot came to the rescue by ordering 10,000 sack

lunches from us. He even told me that he was going to personally eat one so it "better be good."

To the public, it seemed like the City of Dallas was paying for the lunches. In fact, though, Ross Perot sprang for the lunch tab in addition to a huge picnic for the soldiers that same weekend. No one gave Mr. Perot the credit and he never came forth to brag about these generous acts that cost him tens of thousands of dollars.

That's the kind of man Ross Perot is.

It goes without saying that when he ran for President, I supported him 100 percent. Mr. Perot is an outstanding businessman who has a very big heart. So, lo and behold, when "60 Minutes" came to Dallas to do a story on Mr. Perot, they came to see me. Like I said, I'm known as a local Republican and Mr. Perot has been a regular at one of our barbecue joints. I enjoyed being interviewed by correspondent Morley Safer, who ended up eating at Dickey's but asked for some kind of New York bread instead of our hamburger buns. We substituted Texas toast when we made his sandwich but it wasn't what he was used to. The good part is that he loved our beef and sauce.

DICKEY'S BARBECUE

Since ★ 1941

HOWDY

neighbor

SUPER DELICIOUS DESSERTS AND DRINKS

Chocolate Fudge Cake

This was Martha Dickey's traditional birthday cake and is still a favorite with our family.

Serves 12

2 cups flour
2 cups sugar
½ cup (1 stick) butter
½ cup Crisco
4 tablespoons cocoa
½ cup buttermilk
1 tablespoon baking soda
2 eggs
1 teaspoon vanilla extract
1 teaspoon cinnamon

Fudge Icing
½ cup (1 stick) butter
4 tablespoons cocoa
6 tablespoons whole milk
1 (16-ounce) box powdered sugar
1 teaspoon vanilla extract
1 cup chopped pecans

Preheat the oven to 400 degrees F.

Sift together the flour and sugar and set aside.

In a saucepan or double boiler, bring the butter, Crisco, and cocoa to a boil, stirring constantly. Add the butter mixture into the flour and sugar mixture and mix well. In a separate bowl, combine the buttermilk and soda, then stir into the batter. Add the eggs, one at a time, mixing well after each addition, being careful to not overbeat. Stir in the vanilla and cinnamon, and pour the batter into a well-greased (not floured) 11 x 16-inch sheet cake pan. Bake for 20 minutes, or until a toothpick in the middle of the cake comes out with a bit of the fudge still on it. During the last 5 minutes of baking, bring the butter, cocoa, and milk to a boil in a saucepot. Remove from the heat and stir in the powdered sugar, vanilla, and chopped pecans until they are well combined. Ice the cake while it is still hot.

Southern Pecan Pie

Yields 1 (9-inch) pie
Cooking Time: 40 to 50 minutes

1 pre-made graham cracker pie crust
6 tablespoons (¾ stick) unsalted butter
1¼ cups light brown sugar
¾ cup light corn syrup
2 teaspoons vanilla extract
¼ teaspoon kosher salt
3 eggs
2 cups pecan halves

Preheat the oven to 325 degrees F.

Melt the butter in a small heavy saucepan over medium heat. Whisk in the brown sugar until smooth. Remove from the heat and whisk in the corn syrup, vanilla, and salt.

In a separate bowl, lightly beat the eggs, then whisk in the corn syrup mixture. Place the pecan halves in the bottom of the pie shell and pour the corn syrup mixture evenly over the pecans. Place the pie pan on a hot baking sheet and bake for 40 to 50 minutes, or until the filling is set. Allow the pie to cool completely before cutting.

Garnish with as much or as little ice cream as you want!

Not just for kids

One of the things we do at Dickey's to thank our customers is offer them free soft-serve ice cream. It's become a huge hit at our stores throughout the country. But it's kind of funny how ice cream came to be a part of Dickey's.

When my son Roland was a teenager, we went to a food show in Chicago. I can't eat milk products—including ice cream—but I stopped dead in my tracks when I spotted an ice cream mix made of non-dairy, soybean ingredients. It is delicious—fat-free, dairy free, and perfect for anyone watching their waist line.

Pink Lemonade Pie

Yields 1 (9-inch) pie

1 pre-made graham cracker pie crust
1 (6-ounce) can frozen pink lemonade, from concentrate
1 (14-ounce) can Eagle brand condensed milk
1 (8-ounce) container whipped topping, such as Cool Whip

Allow the pink lemonade to melt enough to be able to stir it. Stir together the lemonade, the condensed milk, and the whipped topping thoroughly in a large bowl and pour into the pie crust. Refrigerate for at least 1 hour before slicing and serving. Add whipped topping to taste.

My momma loves any kind of sweet drink—especially lemonade—so naturally we invented this pie.

Aunt Marion's Coffee Cake

This is a great recipe from my Aunt Marion who lives down in Waco, which is just about the center of Texas.

Serves 4 to 6
Cooking Time: 45 to 55 minutes

2 cups all-purpose flour, sifted, plus more for dusting
1 teaspoon baking powder
1 teaspoon ground cinnamon
½ teaspoon salt
⅔ cup unsalted butter, plus more for the pan
1 cup sugar
½ cup brown sugar, packed
2 eggs
1 cup buttermilk

Topping
½ cup brown sugar, packed
½ teaspoon ground cinnamon
¼ teaspoon ground nutmeg

Grease a 9 x 13-inch pan with butter and dust with flour.

In a separate bowl, sift together the flour, baking powder, cinnamon, and salt. Set aside.

In another bowl, cream the butter, sugar, and brown sugar together for 2 to 3 minutes, or until it becomes light and fluffy. Add one egg and beat well, then add the second egg and beat. Add half of the dry ingredients to the egg mixture and stir. Add ½ cup buttermilk, and mix well. Repeat, alternately using the remaining dry ingredients and buttermilk, and stir until smooth. Pour the batter into the floured baking pan.

In a small bowl, mix the brown sugar, cinnamon, and nutmeg for the topping. Sprinkle the topping mixture evenly over the batter. Cover the pan and refrigerate for 8 hours, or overnight.

When you are ready to bake, preheat the oven to 350 degrees F. Remove the pan from the refrigerator, uncover, and bake for 45 to 55 minutes, or until a toothpick inserted into the center of the cake comes out clean. Cut into squares and serve with hot coffee.

Tequila Chocolate Pudding Cake

Serves 8 to 10

½ cup flour
2 teaspoons baking powder
¼ teaspoon salt
¾ cup granulated sugar
¼ cup brewed black coffee
¼ cup coffee tequila
1 ounce chocolate, melted
2 tablespoons (¼ stick) butter, melted
½ cup milk
2 ounces brown sugar
2 ounces powdered sugar
3 tablespoons cocoa powder

Preheat the oven to 350 degrees F.

Sift together the flour, baking powder, and salt. Stir in the sugar, coffee, tequila, melted chocolate, and melted butter. Whisk in the milk until the batter is smooth. Pour the batter into a buttered 9 x 13-inch ovenproof dish. In separate layers, sprinkle the brown sugar, powdered sugar and cocoa over mixture.

Pour ½ cup cold water into a baking pan and set the cake dish into the pan. Bake for 1 hour.

Let the pudding cool for 1 hour, but do not refrigerate. Serve with whipped cream or ice cream.

Anything that has coffee tequila in it is a winning combination with me!

Olive Oil Cookies

This is an old favorite from Cullen Dickey for easy cookies on the weekend. They're a little healthier than most cookies. Lately, we have been experimenting with the addition of cayenne pepper to spice them up (I add ½ teaspoon). Give it a try for something really interesting!

Serves 12

2½ cups flour
½ teaspoon baking powder
1 teaspoon kosher salt
1 cup sugar
2 large eggs
½ cup extra virgin olive oil, plus
    more to grease the cookie sheets
¾ cup soy milk
1 teaspoon vanilla extract

Preheat the oven to 375 degrees F.

Grease two non-stick cookie sheets with extra virgin olive oil. Stir the flour, baking powder, salt, sugar, eggs, olive oil, soy milk, and vanilla together in a large mixing bowl. (Add a touch more soy milk if the mixture seems too dry.) Drop teaspoon-size balls of the cookie dough onto the cookie sheets, spacing them 2 inches apart. Bake the cookies for 13 to 15 minutes, or until they are light brown in color.

Remove from the oven and allow the cookies to cool for 10 minutes on the cookie sheets before transferring them to a serving plate.

S'More Moonies

Yields 9

1 package frozen peanut butter cookie dough, or store-bought cookies
3 blocks bark chocolate
3 graham crackers, finely chopped
9 large, or 18 small, marshmallows
5 Hershey's chocolate bars

Bake the peanut butter cookies according to the package instructions, or buy store bought. Prepare the bark chocolate according to package instructions, and keep warm. Break up the graham crackers into tiny pieces, and set aside in a bowl. Place 1 marshmallow onto a metal skewer, and roast over a fire until the marshmallow begins to turn brown at the edges.

To build your Moonie, start with a peanut butter cookie, then cover with a piece of Hershey's chocolate, then a roasted marshmallow, then top it off with another peanut butter cookie. Place the Moonies on a sheet tray. Drizzle the bark chocolate over the Moonies and sprinkle them with graham cracker pieces. Let the chocolate cool and harden before serving.

I have a sweet tooth and when Big Momma and I go out with a few other couples, I talk them into ordering three or four desserts so I can have a bite of every sweet thing on the menu.

Texas Stout Cake

A friend of mine that owns a booth at the Texas state fair gave me this recipe years ago. It's an old Texas dessert.

Serves 8 to 10
Cooking Time: 45 to 60 minutes

Batter
16 ounces stout lager, such as Shiner Black
10 tablespoons (1 ¼ sticks) unsalted butter, plus more for baking pan
½ cup dark chocolate
½ cup unsweetened cocoa
2 cups brown sugar
½ cup sour cream
2 large eggs
1 tablespoon vanilla extract
2 cups all-purpose flour
2 ½ teaspoons baking soda

Topping
1¼ cups powdered sugar
8 ounces cream cheese, room temperature
½ cup heavy cream

Preheat the oven to 350 degrees F. Butter a 9-inch spring-form pan and line it with parchment paper. Heat the beer and butter in a large saucepan over medium-low heat until the butter melts, then remove from the heat. Add the chocolate, cocoa, and brown sugar and whisk well to blend. Set aside.

In a small bowl, combine the sour cream, eggs, and vanilla and mix well. Add this to the beer mixture. Add the flour and baking soda, and whisk again until smooth. Pour the batter into the buttered pan and bake for 45 minutes to 1 hour, or until the cake has risen and is firm. Place the cake pan on a wire rack to cool.

To make the topping, put the powdered sugar in a food processor and pulse to break up the lumps. Add the cream cheese and blend until smooth. Add the heavy cream and mix until the topping is smooth and spreadable.

Remove the cake from pan and place it on a platter or cake stand. Ice the top of cake only, so that it resembles a frothy pint of stout.

Texas Two-Step Pudding

Serves 4 to 6

Topping
3 (1.4-ounce) packages milk chocolate
    instant pudding mix
5 cups milk

Crust
¾ cup (1½ sticks) unsalted butter, softened
1½ cups all-purpose flour
¾ cups chopped pecans

Filling
8 ounces cream cheese, softened
1 cup powdered sugar
½ container (4 ounces) whipped topping,
    such as Cool Whip

Garnish
Shaved chocolate
Chopped pecans

Actually, this is more of a three-step pudding, but it's a traditional dessert that has been called the Texas Two-Step for as long as I remember. Maybe this is because it's so good it makes you want to dance!

Make the topping first to give it time to chill in the refrigerator. Mix the chocolate pudding with the milk and refrigerate for 4 to 6 hours, or until it sets up.

Preheat the oven to 375 degrees F. To make the crust, mix the softened butter, flour, and chopped pecans together, and spread evenly into a 9 x 13-inch baking pan. Bake for 15 minutes. Set aside, and let cool.

Whisk the cream cheese and the powdered sugar together until it is smooth. Fold in the Cool Whip and spread the mixture over the crust layer. Spread the chocolate pudding topping over the cream cheese layer.

Garnish with shaved chocolate or chopped pecans and serve.

Paige's Banana Pudding

Paige Blackorby works with me at Dickey's Barbecue and has done all the typing on this manuscript. She has also given me ideas and reminded me of a lot of the recipes I needed to include. When Paige has a boyfriend over for dinner, and she needs an emergency dessert, she likes to whip up this shortcut recipe for banana pudding.

Serves 8 to 10

2 boxes Jello vanilla pudding (not instant,
   use the kind that's cooked on the stove)
Half-and-half, according to pudding box instructions
2 teaspoons vanilla extract
2 whole bananas, sliced
1 box vanilla wafers

Cook the pudding according to the directions, but substitute half-and-half for the milk. I like to use a double boiler for this as opposed to putting it over direct heat.

When the custard is cooked, stir in the vanilla extract and set aside to cool to room temperature.

While the custard is cooling, line a Pyrex baking dish or glass bowl with vanilla wafers and bananas, pour the custard over the wafers, and repeat with another layer of bananas and vanilla wafers, and finish with another layer of custard on top.

If you think your guests or significant other wants a richer dessert, I recommend buying canned ready-made whipped cream for the topping. Don't buy the frozen stuff.

Edna's Bread Pudding

This recipe is from a character in my radio commercials and YouTube videos: Joanna Windham (Edna). She is a character alright, which you will come to realize if you ever see her on YouTube, but she also has an incredible sweet tooth. This is one of her favorite recipes.

Serves 8 to 10

1 loaf French bread (preferably a day old)
4 cups half-and-half
3 large eggs, beaten
2 cups sugar
3 tablespoons vanilla extract
1 tablespoon ground cinnamon
1 teaspoon nutmeg
Butter, to coat baking pan

Rum Sauce
½ cup (1 stick) butter
1 cup sugar
½ cup rum

Tear the bread into small pieces and place them in a large bowl. Pour in the half-and-half and allow the bread soak for 30 to 40 minutes. Stir occasionally to mix well. The bread will have a pudding-like consistency. In a separate bowl, beat the eggs and sugar together. Stir the egg mixture into the soaked bread, then add the vanilla, cinnamon, and nutmeg.

Preheat the oven to 350 degrees F.

Gently coat the inside of a baking pan with softened butter. (I like to use a 9 x 13-inch Pyrex baking dish, not a metallic pan.) Pour the pudding mixture into the dish and bake for 1 hour and 15 minutes. A knife inserted in the center of the pudding should come out clean.

I like to eat this dish as it is. Other people like to top it with whipped cream or rum sauce. To make the rum sauce, melt the butter in a small saucepan, then add the sugar and rum. Stir until the mixture is smooth, then spread the sauce over the bread pudding before serving.

Note: If the sauce has too much of an alcohol taste, cut down on the rum.

Elizabeth's Pumpkin Chiffon Pie

Serves 6
Cooking Time: 7 to 10 minutes

Pumpkin Filling
1 package plain gelatin
2/3 cup brown sugar
1/2 teaspoon salt
1/2 teaspoon cinnamon
1/2 teaspoon nutmeg
1/2 teaspoon ground ginger
1 1/4 cups canned pumpkin
3 egg yolks
1/2 cup milk
Sweetened whipped cream

Meringue
3 egg whites
1/2 cup sugar

1 pre-baked pie crust

This is a family favorite. My sister Elizabeth Mills is the best cook within the entire Dickey family, beyond a doubt. That is something, considering all the people in our family are good cooks. When she makes her pumpkin chiffon pie at Christmas and Thanksgiving, I save room for it.

Mix all of the filling ingredients together in a double boiler, bring to a gentle boil, and stir until the mixture thickens. Remove from the heat and allow the pan to cool in a cold water bath until the filling forms loose mounds.

To make the meringue, whip together the egg whites and sugar until the meringue becomes stiff.

Fold the pumpkin filling into the meringue and refrigerate for 2 to 3 hours.

Serve in a pre-baked pie crust and garnish with whipped cream.

Southern Sun Tea

In Texas we have a lot of sunshine throughout the long summer days, so we like to brew tea using the warmth from the sun to make the best brew possible.

Yields 1 gallon

1 gallon water
3 to 4 black tea bags

Fill a 1-gallon airtight jug with water. Either tie the tea bag strings on the handle of the jug top, or lay them over the edge, and screw the lid on over them tightly. The bags should be suspended in the water. Sit the jug outside in the best sunlight, and let it brew. It should take from 2 to 3 hours, depending on how strong you like your tea.

For the best glass of sun tea, fill a large glass full of ice cubes, add a heaping tablespoon of sugar (depending on how sweet you like it), and pour the hot tea over the ice. Add a squeeze of lemon and enjoy!

The (Proper) Michelada

Serves 1

Salt-and-Pepper Mix
2 tablespoons kosher salt
¼ teaspoon coarse ground pepper
¼ teaspoon Tony Chachere's Creole Seasoning

Michelada
Juice of 1 lime
3 ounces spicy V8 juice
2 teaspoons Worcestershire sauce
½ teaspoon Tabasco sauce
1 teaspoon soy sauce
1 bottle Mexican light beer (Sol or Dos Equis)
Kosher salt, to taste
Coarse ground black pepper, to taste

Dip the rim of a beer glass in the juice of a lime, then gently dip the rim of the glass in the salt-and-pepper mix to coat.

In a separate glass, mix the V8 juice, Worcestershire sauce, Tabasco, and soy sauce. Slowly pour the ice-cold beer into the salt-rimmed glass and add the V8 mixture. Season with salt and pepper to taste and serve.

Bloody Mary

Yields 6 drinks

12 ounces Tito's Vodka, or your favorite
24 ounces Clamato
3 beef bouillon cubes
3 tablespoons Worcestershire sauce
½ teaspoon celery salt
1 teaspoon Tabasco sauce
Juice of 4 limes
1 tablespoon jalapeño juice
⅛ teaspoon hickory liquid smoke
Kosher salt, to taste
Coarse ground pepper, to taste

Garnishes
(Choose your two favorites and
    serve on a toothpick)
Pickled green beans
Celery sticks
Pickled carrots
Pickled jalapeños
Spanish olives

Mix everything except the salt, pepper, and garnishes in a pitcher. When you serve, pour it over ice cubes, salt and pepper to taste, and serve each glass with your favorite garnish.

Dreamsicle Mimosa

Yields 8 to 10 drinks

2½ cups fresh squeezed orange juice
Zest of 1 orange
3 ounces Grand Marnier
1 teaspoon clear vanilla extract
1 cup half-and-half
1 cup superfine sugar
1 bottle Brut Champagne
4 to 6 strawberries, washed and halved

This is a fancy dessert drink. In fact, it's too fancy just to be a drink—it's really more of a dessert. Try it, you'll love it!

Blend the orange juice, zest, Grand Marnier, vanilla extract, half-and-half, and sugar in a blender for 30 seconds, or until the sugar has dissolved. Pour the mixture into a metal pan and freeze until hard, 5 hours or overnight. Remove the frozen orange mixture from the freezer and let it sit for 10 minutes to allow it to soften slightly.

Using an ice cream scoop, place 1 small scoop into each Champagne glass. Slowly fill the glass with Champagne and serve garnished with strawberries.

Cucumber-Minted Gin Julep

This is a refined version of the 1862 drink.

Serves 1

1½ tablespoons sugar
5 to 7 cucumber slices, ⅛-inch slice
⅛ cup crushed ice
8 to 10 mint leaves
3 ounces Bombay Sapphire dry gin
2 ounces water

Garnish
Mint sprig
Cucumber slice
Club soda (optional)

Combine the sugar, cucumber slices, ice, and mint leaves in a martini shaker. Using a pestle, smash the ingredients inside the shaker for 10 seconds. Add the gin and water, and place the top tightly on the shaker. Shake for 20 seconds. Pour the Julep into a clean bar glass, straining out all the solids. Garnish the glass with a sprig of mint and a cucumber slice and top it off with club soda, if you desire.

Lemon Drop Martini

Yields 4 drinks

⅓ cup simple syrup
12 ounces citron vodka
3 ounces sweet & sour
1 lemon, sliced into 6 wedges
2 tablespoons sugar

To make a simple syrup, combine 2 parts sugar and one part water and stir to combine.

Combine all the ingredients except the lemon wedges and 2 tablespoons sugar in a large mixing cup or shaker filled with crushed ice. Squeeze in the lemon juice from all 6 wedges, then toss in the wedges, too, and shake the cup like crazy. Pour the sugar onto a flat plate and dip the rims of chilled martini glasses first into water and then into the sugar to coat. Gently strain the martinis into sugar-rimmed, chilled martini glasses, leaving the lemon wedges and ice in the cup. There will be some lemon pulp and possibly ice shavings in the martini—don't worry, this is PERFECT!

Remove the lemon wedges and coat them in the remaining sugar in the plate. Cut a slit in the sugared lemon wedge and set on each martini rim to garnish.

Paige's Wedding Cake Martini

We originally named this recipe after a friend of ours who we know is looking for a husband. Unfortunately, she hasn't found one yet, but some lucky man out there is missing a great martini!

Serves 1

3 ounces vanilla vodka
1 ounce raspberry liquor
1 ounce amaretto liquor
1 ounce pineapple juice

Combine all the ingredients in a mixing cup or shaker filled with ice. Shake like hell. Strain the liquid into a chilled martini glass, leaving the ice in the cup. The martini will be a little frothy, and that's a good thing. Enjoy!

Martini

Every winter I travel to Florida to get my old bones away from snow and ice—or if Big Momma is on a terror, I go to hide out. My neighbors in Florida are Susan and Warren Trilling. Susan is a great martini-Maker and makes them every kind of way! This is one of her best.

Serves 1

2 ounces vodka
½ ounce Italian vermouth
1 tablespoon olive juice
2 blue cheese-stuffed olives

Add the vodka, vermouth, and olive juice to a martini shaker with ½ cup cracked ice. Shake until nice and cold and strain into a chilled martini glass. Add the blue cheese olives and serve with toothpicks.

Note: Certain specialty and liquor stores carry the blue cheese olives. This way you are getting your vitamins and protein along with your alcohol! At least, that's my story and I'm sticking to it.

DICKEY'S BARBECUE
Since ★ 1941
HOWDY
neighbor

INDEX

Acknowledgments

If I had a dollar for everyone who has suggested that the Dickey family come up with a cookbook, I'd certainly be a rich man. A cookbook is a project I've been pondering for years but I just wasn't sure how I wanted to do it. Then one day I was strolling through a Florida bookstore and happened upon a cookbook that seemed to be the spittin' image of how I wanted mine to be. This book was overflowing with all the ingredients that I had dreamed about mixing up—tasty recipes, lots of stories and plenty of family pictures. I also wanted my book to be two parts cooking tips, a dash of philosophy and a sprinkling of entertaining advice.

With the help of way too many folks to name, I think I've accomplished all that and more with Mr. Dickey's Barbecue Cookbook. I hate to list my helpers and advisors who walked me through this project because that will open myself up to leaving somebody out and getting me into all sorts of trouble, but let me tell you I'm accustomed to that. I just can't go any further without thanking a few people who got me started, revved up my engine and rode with me to the finish line.

Obviously, Dickey's Barbecue wouldn't have gotten off the ground if it hadn't been for my hard-working parents—my mother, Ollie Dickey, and my Dad, Travis Dickey Sr. who had the idea for Dickey's in the first place.

I really can't name all the people I owe a huge thanks, but I must thank the great team who helped me literally put this book together... so I tip my hat to a great co-author Polly, for taming my stories just enough to be publishable; to a first-rate editor Janice, for sound advice and reining me in whenever needed; to a a great chef, Jeff Forrester, who doubles as Dickey's director of purchasing and didn't think twice about jumping in to review all my recipes and truly double check everything; and last but not least, project manager extraordinare Paige Blackorby, who is a brand manager on Dickey's marketing team by day and had the very thankless task of trying to manage me and this book. Without Paige this book would be nothing more than notes on a tape recorder and scribbles on a fax.

Of course, Dickey's wouldn't be number one in my opinion if it weren't for a talented team of hardworking employees and dedicated franchise owners.

Last but not least, I am forever grateful to Dickey's loyal customers—the people who have patronized our stores through the years—and have made us what we are today. Without these folks to pass the word about our great food and unforgettable service, Dickey's would never be the smashing success that it is today.

Thanks for everything, y'all! Enjoy the Dickey's story and be sure to visit one of our stores soon!